W9-AQT-728

Twayne's English Authors Series

Sylvia E. Bowman, *Editor*

INDIANA UNIVERSITY

Dante Gabriel Rossetti

Since 1928, the centenary of his birth, an increasing number of biographies and studies have appeared about Dante Gabriel Rossetti. One result of these has been to continue a disunified and often conflicting view of the man. These studies have been mostly biographical. Even in those particular articles and books that have examined Rossetti's work, there has been no attempt to trace any continuing line of thematic development.

This book concerns itself with that aim. It proposes that from the outset Rossetti concerned himself with his personal quest after Love, as he idealized it in Woman. His early art and writings are influenced significantly by Dante's *Vita Nuova,* with Beatrice as symbol of Love, found and etherealized. From this initial vision of the spiritualized Love dream, through to the final depictions of Woman in his late poems, tales, and art as the Circean *femme fatale,* the evolution of Rossetti's artistic expression is clearly revealed.

Like Blake before him, Rossetti speaks in both poetry and art; and, like Blake again, he emerges a figure not closely identified with his century. In the world of Tractarianism, the Crimean War, Darwinian evolution, and significant political and economic changes, Rossetti stands uncommitted, detached. Unlike many of his contemporaries, such as Tennyson, whose conception of art was didactic, Rossetti stimulated the new aestheticism to follow. In an age so haunted by writers who sought to re-affirm their nineteenth century God, Rossetti pursued a vision of his own, a vision imbued with an identity rooted in the world of the gothic, the medieval, the troubadour. To understand this world is to further enrich the meaning of "Victorian."

Dante Gabriel Rossetti

By ROBERT D. JOHNSTON
University of West Florida

Twayne Publishers, Inc. :: New York

Library of Congress Catalog Card Number: 71-81534

MANUFACTURED IN THE UNITED STATES OF AMERICA

Preface

DANTE GABRIEL ROSSETTI never was at a loss for friends or for foes, either before or after his death in April, 1882. The poetic and the artistic expressions of Rossetti have generated warm defense and equally warm vituperation. The hint of storm clouds on the horizon of Dante Gabriel's career in the criticism of his oil "Ecce Ancilla Domini" (1850) was nothing compared to some observations, about the same time, about Hawthorne's *The Scarlet Letter.* But Rossetti's day also came in 1871 with the "Fleshly School" attack on his *Poems.* Robert Buchanan's abuse was an unnerving splash coming after an otherwise calm tide of panegyric reviews from such critics as William Morris, Algernon Swinburne, Joseph Knight, and Westland Marston.

The result of such criticism from Buchanan and others was that Rossetti withdrew further from public account. Consequently, erroneous evaluations were fostered. What little his contemporaries came to see of his art was unfortunately the late oils with their strange distortions and their sensuous figures. And, in spite of Rossetti's attempt to avoid censure, the many voices of Victorian morality rumbled on. Often, too, particularly after his death, the harsh observations and the unkind comments came from those who had been close to him.

With the centenary of his birth in 1928, the renewed interest in Rossetti's life brought the same divided sentiments. Violet Hunt's study of Elizabeth Siddal in *The Wife of Rossetti* contributed to an already distorted estimation of Dante Gabriel's life. There were at this time, however, some serious attempts to judge fairly both the man and his work, such as Baum's study of *The House of Life* sonnets and Mégroz's examination of the poetry and art. More recently a number of good biographies have appeared, and the number of shorter studies grows each year. Of course Rossetti's brother, William, has made a significant contribution in his numerous editions of Dante Gabriel's poetry and prose and in his collections of family letters and papers. In 1965 two new books appeared: Rosalie Grylls' *Portrait of Rossetti,* and Gale Pedrick's *Life with Rossetti.* Recently, G. H. Fleming's *Rossetti and the PRB* (1967) examines the poet in that important circle. In this wealth of material, most attention has been turned to biographical facts. Some articles have considered separate works and a few longer criticisms have discussed in general the body of Rossetti's expression. However, few of these studies have attempted to trace any lines of thematic development.

The purpose of this volume is to examine closely Rossetti's poetry and art. His poetry is considered in separate groupings: translations and prose work; *The House of Life,* Parts I and II; narrative poems; and final sonnets. Actually Rossetti's writing career seems divided in this way, beginning with the translations and ending with some short academic pieces. His many water colors and oils are discussed within these chapters at the times they were completed, for the poetry and the art reflect the same sources of inspiration.

This division is chronological in pattern; however, I have attempted to trace in these chapters the line of Rossetti's thought, indicating that what he discovered in and nurtured from his early years became the main stimulus operating through his entire career—an attitude that changes from lucid hope to clouded anxiety, and finally to darkened fear. The heightened ideal of the Beatrice figure, engendered from the troubadour poets and from Dante, alters into the voluptuous forms of Lilith and Monna Vanna to become at last the grotesque shape of the fatal Siren. To trace this theme of love in Rossetti is to discover his main voice, and this I have tried to do.

This study does not undertake an examination of the many biographical questions prompted by the complexities and eccentricities of Rossetti's life. Biography is considered insofar as such material expands and illuminates my primary concern—the thematic ideas as they appear in the writings and art. Also, there is no detailed attempt to examine his expressions within the total realm of Victorian events and literature, except wherever it is appropriate to suggest his lack of interest in or commitment to his times, and to indicate his contributions to the Esthetic Movement which came late to the nineteenth century. To attempt a Rossetti biography at this time would be both presumptuous and repetitive, in light of the many recent and full studies. Oswald Doughty's *A Victorian Romantic*, especially, provides most of the material that the reader of a Rossetti biography may need.

My indebtedness to earlier studies such as R. D. Waller's *The Rossetti Family* (1932) and to R. L. Mégroz's *Painter Poet of Heaven in Earth* (1929), as well as to Doughty's biography, is obvious. Holman Hunt's *Pre-Raphaelitism and the Pre-Raphaelite Brotherhood* (1906) is of course a necessary document in understanding the relation of that group in Rossetti's youth.

ROBERT D. JOHNSTON

Pensacola, Florida

DANTE GABRIEL ROSSETTI

Contents

Chronology

1828 Dante Gabriel Rossetti, christened Gabriel Charles Dante Rossetti, born May 12, at No. 38, Charlotte Street, Portland Place, London, second of four children to Gabriele and Frances Polidori Rossetti.

1828–1836 Formative years, before formal schooling in 1836; influenced by his father's Dante studies, numerous family acquaintances, and close family ties. Early in period was sketching and writing.

1836 Schooling begins, first at Paul's, a preparatory day school. In 1837 he goes for four years to King's College School with William.

1841 Leaves King's College. For four years attends Sass's drawing school under F. S. Cary.

1845 In December enters the Antique School of the Royal Academy.

1847 At nineteen begins verse translations from Dante and Dante's contemporaries. Writes "The Blessed Damozel"; begins "My Sister's Sleep," "The Portrait" and "Dante at Verona."

1848 Leaves Royal Academy School. Joins Ford Madox Brown as an art student. Meets Holman Hunt and shares his studio. Pre-Raphaelite Brotherhood formed with John Millais, Holman Hunt, Thomas Woolner, James Collinson, Frederick Stephens, Rossetti, and his brother, William.

1849 Exhibits his "The Girlhood of Mary Virgin" at the Free Exhibition. This first painting is purchased by the Marchioness of Bath. Hunt and Rossetti tour Paris and Belgium. Rossetti settles in studio at 72 Newman Street, London. First edition of *The Germ* appears in late December.

1850 *The Germ*, renamed *Art and Poetry*, fails after four numbers. Pre-Raphaelite Brotherhood (PRB) is attacked after

Rossetti reveals identity of the group. Rossetti vows never to exhibit again following criticism of his "Ecce Ancilla Domini." Meets Elizabeth Siddal.

1851 In May, Ruskin defends the PRB in *The Times*.

1852 Elizabeth Siddal and Rossetti probably engaged in early 1852. Rossetti moves to 14 Chatham Place, near the Blackfriars Bridge.

1853 Early signs of Lizzie's deteriorating health.

1854 Death of Rossetti's father, Gabriele. Spends several months at Hastings with Lizzie to better her health. Rossetti begins his painting "Found." Close relationship with Ruskin begins; begins teaching drawing at Working Men's College.

1855 Ruskin offers Lizzie one hundred and fifty pounds yearly for her drawings; Lizzie visits France for her health. Strife between Rossetti and Ruskin begins.

1856 Hunt returns from Palestine. Rossetti befriends Morris and Edward Burne-Jones. Llandaff triptych is commissioned.

1857 Pre-Raphaelite Exhibition indicates growing power of the movement. "Jovial Campaign" finds Rossetti, William Morris, Edward Jones, Val Prinsep, R. S. Stanhope, Arthur Hughes, and John Pollen working on frescoes in Oxford Union Debating Hall. Swinburne meets Rossetti. Jane Burden becomes Rossetti's model.

1858 "Jovial Campaign" dissolves. Rossetti's money problems increase.

1859 William Morris and Jane Burden are married.

1860 Rossetti and Lizzie married on May 23. Rossetti completes "Bocca Bociata," the beginning of his series of sensuous women-and-flowers oils.

1861 In May, Lizzie delivers a stillborn child. Rossetti publishes his *Early Italian Poets*.

1862 Lizzie dies from effects of overdose of laudanum, February 11. Rossetti buries his manuscript poems with her. Moves to 16 Cheyne Walk.

1863 Rossetti helps complete Gilchrist's *Life of Blake*.

1864 Completes the Llandaff triptych.

1865 Final break in friendship with Ruskin.

1866–1867 Decline begins in Rossetti's health, with hydrocele, insomnia, and concern over eyesight.

1868 Visits Penkill Castle, Ayrshire, with Miss Boyd. Poetic impulse returns in December with the sonnets "Willowwood."

1869 In October, manuscript of Rossetti's early poems retrieved from Lizzie's grave.

1870 Chloral is recommended for insomnia. Stays long at Scalands. *Poems* appears in April, establishing his reputation as poet-artist.

1871 Morris and Rossetti lease jointly Kelmscott Manor. R. W. Buchanan's "Fleshly School of Poetry" attack in October contributes to increasing physical and mental instability.

1872 Mental crisis in June in which Rossetti believes many in a conspiracy against him. Attempts suicide by overdose of laudanum. Returns to Kelmscott for two years.

1874 In July, leaves Kelmscott for last time. Estrangement with Morris; their relation in the "Firm" dissolves.

1875 In October, accompanied by George Hake, leases Aldwick Lodge in Bognor, Sussex.

1876 Dejection and mental degeneration continue, along with increased alcohol and chloral consumption. Returns from Bognor to Cheyne Walk in July.

1877 Seriously ill in May; ordered by doctor out of London; goes to Herne Bay, not to return until early November.

1878–1880 Years of continued enfeebled health and of increased work to attempt allaying increasing debts and to complete unfulfilled commissions. Insomnia intensifies.

1881 Slow, persistent decline in mental and physical health. In August, Hall Caine comes to live with Rossetti at Cheyne Walk. In September, visits the English Lakes. *Ballads and Sonnets* appears along with new edition of *Poems.*

1882 Left arm and hand paralyzed. Goes to Birchington-on-Sea in February. Dies Easter Day, April 9; buried at Birchington.

CHAPTER 1

Rossetti Criticism

THE drawing by Max Beerbohm that serves as frontispiece to his *Rossetti and His Circle* (1922) is interesting for a number of good reasons. For one, it becomes a delightful piece of comic insight into Dante Gabriel Rossetti's world, a place that often has evoked too little humor and too much lugubrious observation. This sketch shows Dante Gabriel as a youngster in his family home in Charlotte Street, London. He lies on the floor, is attired in a painter's smock, and is "precociously manifesting," as Beerbohm explains, while all about him are the strange, wild figures of men in various poses of excitement. We are told they are some of the many exiled patriots of Italy who frequented the Rossetti household. The young boy is completely aloof to the charged atmosphere of political argument. For another reason, Beerbohm's drawing, although its apparent purpose may be humorous, suggests the environment in which Rossetti grew up. In this same picture, Dante Gabriel's old father, Gabriele, sits poring over some papers, probably his own eccentric work on Dante Alighieri.

I *Beerbohm's Insights*

To the young Rossetti children the influence of the Italian poet was deeply felt. As for the omnipresence of politics in his home in these early years, Dante Gabriel paid little heed. His indifference to contemporary matters continued throughout his lifetime as poet and artist. Beerbohm's drawing also hints at the freedom the Rossetti children were permitted. They were encouraged to develop their own talents, and at early ages they turned to writing stories and making sketches. In one way this atmosphere in which they thrived contributed so much to their success as artists, particularly to that of Dante Gabriel and Christina. But in other ways such freedom probably encouraged Dante Gabriel's later laxness in his formal training at the academy schools and in his persistent inability to stay long with a particular task before him.

The other twenty-two sketches by Beerbohm handle various events in the times of Rossetti and his circle of friends, and they culminate with the well-known drawing of Oscar Wilde, holding a lily and lecturing on Rossetti to a group of Quakerish-looking Americans.

As the Beerbohm drawings suggest, Rossetti's life is full of many colorful and dramatic events and facts. There has always been something of an aura of the mysterious and ultimately inexplicable around Rossetti's life, a final evaluation that escapes many biographers and defies being stated in definable terms. Rossetti encouraged some of this elusiveness himself through his own withdrawal from public concerns, through his many eccentricities, and through his own artistic projection. For any artist who pursues the abstract and who fills his expression with a great deal of the supernatural and the Gothic, there will arise a sense of the fleeting image, the blurred conception. That is not to suggest that his final expression is faulty, but only that the critical explanation of his work leaves, at last, something outside the accomplished investigation.

II *Interpretation: Varieties*

Out of the Pre-Raphaelite group, with Rossetti at its center, emerged contributions to art and literature that came to be identified with the Esthetic Movement and with what we understand in our own day as the independence and the peculiarities of the artist. The painter or poet is understood to be one unto himself; he is often and in many ways accepted as unlike the masses of men to whom he speaks. Beerbohm's drawings suggest this "difference" in the Rossetti circle. One natural result of studies about this interesting life of Rossetti is that Dante Gabriel's work and activities, in many ways individualistic, have evoked a variety of interpretations. For a man who was so idiosyncratic in his ways—and many are the stories told of his Blue China, his wombats, and his strange late-night soirees at Cheyne Walk—and whose art and poetry touch so much that is not only un-English but is also unworldly, it is easy to account for the many studies that depict him as peculiar and at last haunted.

Attempts have been made by friends, especially of late by surviving relatives, to set the Rossetti Legend in order. Helen Rossetti Angeli, the niece of Dante Gabriel, remarks about the "posthumous denigration" of Rossetti's name: "We have new names for it . . . the Greeks no doubt had a name for it, and the thing itself is as old as the arts of war and peace, coeval with the building and destruction of temples. The small ambition that cannot build has ever been eager to destroy." [1] And Mrs. Angeli believes that no poet of the language, not even Poe, has been more lied about than Rossetti.

The deprecation began in 1871 with Robert Buchanan's "The Fleshly School of Poetry" attack, a scathing and embittered review of Rossetti's *Poems* (1870) that was later retracted by Buchanan himself. Holman Hunt's two-volume study *Pre-Raphaelitism and the Pre-Raphaelite Brotherhood* (1905) is largely concerned with Hunt's own work, but he manages to question, in fussy hindsight, the misplaced emphasis on Rossetti's role as leader in the Pre-Raphaelite Movement. William Bell Scott in *Autobiographical Notes* (1892) began before Hunt to make unhappy innuendoes about his relationship with Rossetti. The occasion of the centenary of Rossetti's birth in 1928 brought forth a great number of studies and biographies. Hall Caine's *Recollections of Rossetti* appeared, an enlargement of his 1882 work, in which he pleaded that he would correct much of the error perpetrated about Dante Gabriel; but in many ways his book adds fuel to a great body of the sensational that had already developed about Rossetti's name.

It is far too easy to be glib about Rossetti, even when facts seem available to support whatever estimates we wish to make; and Violet Hunt's book is a case in point. Her 1932 *The Wife of Rossetti*, sets out to tell the truth, not about Rossetti, but "about the woman he married." Miss Hunt claims to "have laid bare much that is painful, wild and unexpected" [2]; but R. L. Mégroz, in his excellent study, *Painter Poet of Heaven in Earth*, when referring to Miss Hunt's work on Rossetti and Lizzie Siddal, comments on the many "extravagant vagaries of biographical comment" that Dante Gabriel's "complex and puzzling personality" excited.[3] Mégroz's own critical investigation is one of the first to examine closely the work of Rossetti, and his judgments are both sound and illuminating. No other full-length work attempts exclusively to study Rossetti's poetry and art from their beginnings to the last oils and narrative poems of 1880–1881. R. D. Waller, in *The Rossetti Family* (1932), is concerned only with the early years.

The biography *A Victorian Romantic* (1949) by Oswald Doughty is a careful work that purports, as the author himself states, not to be a critical study of Rossetti's paintings and poetry. What explanations of Rossetti's work that do appear in it are used to illustrate biographical views. Perhaps the chief factor of Rossetti's life that Doughty demonstrates is the Rossetti-Mrs. Morris love relationship. This contention has been challenged since the letters from Rossetti to Mrs. Morris were recently released for examination; for Rosalie Grylls, in her biography, *Portrait of Rossetti* (1964), insists that no evidence supports this assertion by Doughty, Caine, and others.[4] Aside from this point of controversy, around which a great deal of biographical evaluation revolves, Doughty's book is indeed complete and balanced. The old argument from Rossetti admirers, that he had not been fairly judged because too often his kinder and more generous attributes were overlooked, cannot be so quickly charged against Doughty. For anyone interested in the life of Rossetti, this biography is most necessary.

Rosalie Grylls's *Portrait of Rossetti* and Gale Pedrick's *Life with Rossetti* (1964) are only some of the more recent studies of the poet-painter. Miss Grylls's book includes the important letters between Dante Gabriel and Janey Morris that were released by the British Museum in January, 1965. Also interesting is the fact that Miss Grylls understands the role in and impact on Rossetti's life of Elizabeth Siddal. When we study Dante Gabriel's poetry and art throughout his career, the role of woman is discovered to be an important but changing one. In this most recent study, Miss Grylls regards Rossetti's love for Elizabeth Siddal as "an insidious cancer in his spirits." This attitude is not new, but it is different because of its rare appearance.

Usually Lizzie is seen as the awakening of love and as the perpetuator of Rossetti's love dream after her death. This conception of her, Doughty and others insist, has given rise to the mistaken notion that Rossetti wrote his *The House of Life* with her primarily in mind. What is discovered in an examination of Rossetti's work is that she, like other women, becomes the love ideal finally turned awry. She becomes the manifestation in this world for Rossetti of what he hoped to discover in the life beyond; but, like all dreams sought out in reality, her image at last emerges in his poems and art as a grotesque, misshapen figure.

The Pedrick study examines the relationship between Henry Treffry Dunn and Rossetti that had been treated in Dunn's *Recollections of Rossetti and His Circle* (1904). Pedrick, great-nephew of Dunn, gives an interesting account of how Dunn became Rossetti's confidant during his long stay with Rossetti at Cheyne Walk. Dunn was supposedly Rossetti's assistant who eventually with great fidelity painted replicas of many of Rossetti's pictures; but, as time went on, Dunn assumed many duties in the administration of Rossetti's household. Pedrick, using some new letters from a large collection of family materials, presents a picture of life at Cheyne Walk with the intention of providing what he says is "a better answer than do the speculations of some who might have been kinder in their assessments." [5]

The most complete and probably the fairest evaluation of Rossetti to date is Doughty's. The 1929 study by Mégroz is still the only one that tries to examine fully Dante Gabriel's work, but the approach is not a chronological one with any intention of following lines of artistic development. Paull Baum considered in 1928 the sonnet sequence *The House of Life;* but, as Waller was to insist a few years later, Baum does not examine these one hundred two poems in relation to the influence of Dante. Not to be forgotten too is that Rossetti was, like Blake before him, both poet and painter; and both artistic modes must be seen in some relationship. Although Rossetti's own interest shifted at various times in his creative years from a primary concern for painting to writing poetry, his double interests always reflect each other. The beautiful and reliable study of Dante Gabriel's art by H. C. Marillier (1899) is an invaluable aid in examining Rossetti's water-color and oil work in this relationship.[6]

For those interested in focusing on his poetry and art as a means of evaluating and understanding Rossetti's endeavors, there are a number of apparent and inescapable problems. First, to interpret the art and poems as expressions separate from his life and the circumstances of his time might be desirable in an attempt to avoid trying to justify his biography; but such an approach would indeed, with Rossetti at least, depreciate the validity of such findings. Second, the temptation to read through these works into his personal activities presents its own difficulty.

Doughty occasionally, in his desire to establish some biographical point, pushes his interpretation of some poem or art piece where it seems least desirous to go. Furthermore, to attempt a middle path between these alternatives can be a frustrating undertaking; for what Rossetti believed and what he often lived appeared directly in his work.

III *Dante and the Concept of Love*

Rossetti's peculiar outlook on love that is the force welding his expression together was acted out in his relations with the many women in his life—the fleshly and often coarse Fanny Cornforth; the sickly, often cantankerous Elizabeth Siddal with her suggestion of the spiritual; and Mrs. Janey Morris, who for Rossetti unquestionably seemed to be a composite of so many of the others. The distance that Rossetti traveled, both as man and artist, from early to late creative years can be seen partly in looking at his poems "Blessed Damozel" and "The Orchard Pit" together, as well as at his paintings "Beata Beatrix" and his last "Salutation of Beatrice." This comparison is not lightly suggested or quickly conceived; for, if we make a careful inspection of the poems and art from early attempts to later expressions, we find the threads of development appearing.

Rossetti's style and subject matter in his art work and in his poetry are truly varied. He began with his chaste religious oils, and then he conceived and executed many exquisite water colors before again going back in his maturity to oils for his sumptuous depictions of what his brother, William, with whimsical precision, called "female heads with floral adjuncts." Rossetti's poetry also begins with a clarity that later on, particularly in his *The House of Life* sonnets, is often lost in tortured complexity. But Dante Gabriel finally returned to a plainer language that promised strength.

Both art and writing also reflect common stimuli, and the central body of his expression indicates the powerful influence of Dante. Unlike the more recognizable effects from such artists as Browning, Poe, or the Italian troubadour poets, the work of Dante, particularly the *Vita Nuova*, was more pervasive and subtle. The influence was part of Rossetti's heredity, so that what he had received became something quite peculiarly his own.

CHAPTER 2

Two Worlds

ALMOST all critics who have examined Rossetti's thought, as well as his biography, have noted the disparity between his two central worlds of the flesh and the spirit. But what is of utmost concern is that this disparity is the key to his poetry and his art. R. D. Waller speaks of this fact in his excellent study of the Rossettis: "The warring elements within him which brought his life to such depths of misery and remorse as few poets have plumbed, are symbolized by the opposite poles of literary inspiration. . . ." [1] And Oswald Doughty indicates the same idea when he writes that Rossetti's life and art were dominated by a dream, and that not to recognize this fact is to find "his art and life . . . scarcely comprehensible." [2]

I *"My Father's Devoted Studies"*

The dream issued primarily from Dante and his *Vita Nuova,* a writer and a work that had a profound impact on Rossetti because his father, Gabriele, had devoted long years of conscientious study to Dante. Gabriele had come to London in 1824, a political refugee fleeing Ferdinand IV of Naples, who had abolished the new constitution established not long before and was destroying his enemies. Gabriele had supported the rebels against Ferdinand in the revolution of 1820; and, when Ferdinand, with Austrian help reasserted his power, Gabriele was assisted in his escape from Italy by an English fleet in the Bay of Naples under the command of Sir Graham Moore.

Gabriele began his Dante publications in 1825, and his work of love continued until his death in 1854. In his preface to the 1861 edition of *Early Italian Poets,* Dante Gabriel speaks of the influence on him of his father's studies: "The first associations I have are connected with my father's devoted studies. . . . Thus, in those early days, all around me partook of the influence of the great Florentine; till, from viewing it as a natural element, I also, growing older, was drawn within the circle."[3]

But where Gabriele found in Dante, in his cryptic and involved reading, a support for his own anti-papist views, the young son, Dante Gabriel, found the mysteries of Dante's Love. In his sonnet on the *Vita Nuova* (1852), Dante Gabriel speaks of his discovery:

> . . . I, long bound within the threefold charm
> Of Dante's love sublimed to heavenly mood,
> Had marvelled, touching his Beatitude
> . . . .
> At length within this book I found pourtrayed
> Newborn that Paradisal Love of his,
> And simple like a child; with whose clear aid
> I understood.

Rossetti's attempt to maintain his vision of "Paradisal Love" was the impetus behind much of his expression. Yet it was not the Paradise of Dante's *Divine Comedy* that caught Rossetti's imagination and sympathy, but, as Mégroz[4] remarks, Rossetti's concern was with the Dante "whose spiritual home was the Purgatory . . . whose aspirations came to birth with the experience described in the 'New Life.'" Rossetti was twenty when he completed the translation of *Vita Nuova,* a superb achievement that, as others have attested, speaks of the power the original held over the young man who was not to meet his Beatrice until 1850. If Dante's Paradise appeared at all in Rossetti's expression, it did so in his early pictures as "The Girlhood of Mary Virgin" (1849) and "Ecce Ancilla Domini" (1850) and in such poems as "Annunciation" (1847) and "Ave" (1847).

The years 1847–1850 were eventful, exciting ones for Rossetti. He had entered the Antique School of the Royal Academy in December, 1845, after having attended Sass's drawing school for four years; but at the Academy he was disappointed and uninterested. The discipline annoyed him, and he was more interested in writing love poems and in making translations from Dante and his contemporaries; in 1847 he had begun "The Blessed Damozel" and "My Sister's Sleep." Rossetti records himself in his prose piece "St. Agnes of Intercession" (1850) that his own original drawings far outnumbered his school drawings, and that these were original sketches with medieval settings, often of knights and fair ladies, into which themes of "Paradisal Love" had been projected. In early 1848 he left the Academy, escaping the academic concern "rigidly exact and dealing often with trifles." He was often later frustrated because of his failure to master the necessary art fundamentals while at the Antique School.

The insistent desire to pursue subjects of his own choosing in art, usually at the expense of the technicalities he should have mastered, was again apparent in Rossetti's dissatisfaction in 1848 with his pupil-teacher relationship with Ford Madox Brown, who had so generously agreed to take without fee the young, inexperienced artist into his own studio. All too soon Rossetti found Brown as exacting in his teachings as the Academy School; Brown had set him the task of drawing bottles and jars, and Gabriel gave it up with his usual lack of discipline and persistence. At the Royal Academy Exhibition in 1848 Rossetti saw Holman Hunt's "Eve of St. Agnes," called on the art student, and began a new close friendship. From Brown, Gabriel drifted to Hunt; and, under Hunt's supervision, he began his first significant oil, "The Girlhood of Mary Virgin."

II *The Pre-Raphaelite Brotherhood*

From this new relationship came the impetus behind the Pre-Raphaelite Brotherhood. Hunt, excited about Pre-Raphaelite detail and a return to Nature, and rebellious against much of contemporary art as well as against Raphael, stirred Rossetti and John Millais, who—both mainly uninterested in abstract principles—acquiesced. Into this limited circle of young rebellious art students Gabriel brought his brother, William; Thomas Woolner, a student sculptor; and James Collinson, an unpromising painter. Hunt brought into the expanding group his own pupil, Frederick Stephens.

The eventful meeting at Millais' studio among these seven over a book of engravings by Lasinio of the fourteenth-century frescoes of the Campo Santo in Pisa is well known. Thus in September, 1848, the Brotherhood group came into being. Nevertheless, the Brotherhood was never a unified group; for their principles and viewpoints differed. Hunt alone was perhaps sincere and earnest in his desire to bring art back to the fidelity of nature. For Gabriel, the meetings were largely an opportunity for pleasure since he lacked at this time any guiding principles or philosophical goals—a state that was to be true throughout the remainder of his career. Aside from Rossetti's few important art works in these early years that attempt a conforming religious approach, most of the religious sense that Gabriel may have found in Dante was confused and thus transformed into the nebulous "Paradisal Love" he sought for and perhaps only temporarily found later, as is revealed in some sonnets of 1868–1871.

Mégroz[5] remarks that the wonder is not that the Brotherhood dissolved so readily but that it lasted the few years it did. The first major showing of its work was in the spring of 1849 when Hunt and Millais exhibited at the Academy; and Rossetti, without informing the other two artists, sent his "Girlhood of Mary Virgin" to the Free Exhibition. Not until Rossetti later revealed the meaning of the PRB initials to Alexander Munro did the Brotherhood art come under caustic attack in 1850. Gabriel's oil "Ecce Ancilla Domini," when presented at the Free Exhibition, was called puerile and sold only after a long delay. After this experience Rossetti abandoned religious themes, and his Dantesque subjects were as close as he came to "religion" in the future. In the next few years he completed a number of important water colors from Dante, such as his "Beatrice Denying Her Salutation" (1851) and "Dante Drawing the Angel" (1853). His poem "Dante at Verona" was begun in 1848, and the sonnet on the *Vita Nuova* (1852) attests, as we have noted, to the power that Dante exercised over him.

The PRB magazine *The Germ,* urged upon the group by Rossetti, appeared only four times with an altered title of *Art and Poetry* for the third and fourth numbers in 1850. To these numbers Gabriel contributed eleven poems and two prose pieces, "Hand and Soul" and "St. Agnes of Intercession." The aims of the publication, announced in the first number, are vaguely presented. And it was not until after Coventry Patmore urged John Ruskin to defend the Brotherhood in two letters to *The Times* in May, 1851, that some clear-cut principles emerged.

Ruskin's help came to the group at a crucial time. The PRB had been under attack from many influential periodicals, such as the *Athenaeum* and *The Times,* once the meaning of their initials was revealed. The English public interpreted "PRB" to mean an open attack on not only Raphael but all of contemporary British art. The many abusive accusations from the press—charges of blasphemy, popery, and crudity—were intensely disconcerting to the young artist-rebels; and in the spring of 1851 they sought outside support. Millais, whose work had been particularly attacked, begged Patmore, friend to the PRB, to approach Ruskin. Such a choice for assistance was understandable. Ruskin's *Modern Painters* had earlier inspired the Brotherhood. As a result of his defense, the furor gradually subsided, and by the fall of 1851 the Pre-Raphaelite movement took on the semblance of stability and respectability.

III *Lizzie Siddal—"Beatrice Found"*

In the midst of these attacks on the Brotherhood, Dante Gabriel had met and fallen in love with Elizabeth Siddal. Walter Deverell, a member of the group gathering about the Brotherhood, had introduced Lizzie to Rossetti; and she appears in Rossetti's work for the first time in his water color "Rossovestita" (1850); she was a dominant force in his thought and expression until her death in 1862. Until their meeting, Rossetti had lived in a dream of idealized love that knew as yet none of the ugliness and despair of actuality. This mystic idealism had permeated his poem "The Blessed Damozel" of a few years before:

> "We two will stand beside that shrine,
> Occult, withheld, untrod
>
> . . . .
>
> "We two will lie i' the shadow of
> That living mystic tree
> Within whose secret growth the Dove
> Is sometimes felt to be. . . ."

The poem is Dantesque, colored through by the romantic medievalism that Rossetti loved and lived in his imagination, the world he found and to which he responded in such favorite poets as Keats. Again, in his "A Prayer" (1848) the same inexperienced voice appears, celebrating a chivalric love he found so abundantly expressed in the Italian poets—Guido Cavalcanti, Cino da Pistoia, and others—he translated:

> Lady, canst thou not guess
> The words which my thoughts seek:
>
> . . . .
>
> Oh thou must know my love is strong,
> Hearing my voice so weak.

His own urgent sex impulses, conflicting with the limitations imposed by a stern moral code taught by his mother, were projected by the young Rossetti into an elevated idealistic concept of love. Sublimated, these emotions appear in part in the youthful interest Rossetti found in the Brotherhood aims; and this elevation of strong desires into esthetic dedications is also sensed in his "Hand and Soul" of 1849.

When Miss Siddal appeared in 1850, she must have come to Gabriel as a fulfillment of his love ideal, materialized in the flesh. Unlike Dante, whose "Paradisal Love," which Rossetti understood and felt so profoundly in *Vita Nuova,* was ultimately chastened and spiritualized in the *Divine Comedy,* Gabriel never seriously followed the Florentine poet beyond his earlier work. As a result, Beatrice remains for Rossetti a symbol of impassioned love exalted through longing to an unobtainable ideal. However, in his relationship with Lizzie from 1850 to 1862, Gabriel must have often sensed the many parallels between his love for her and Dante's love for Beatrice. For Rossetti, Miss Siddal came with much the same feeling of fate and wonder that Dante records in his *Vita Nuova* about the appearance of his beloved. In his translation of this work, Rossetti describes Dante's responses, and thus records his own toward Lizzie: "I say that, from that time forward, Love quite governed my soul . . . with so safe and undisputed a lordship that I had nothing left for it but to do all his bidding continually." The parallel is further recognizable in the death of both Beatrice and Lizzie, each achieving an idealization that Rossetti himself was later to depict in his "Beata Beatrix" (1863). This oil, Rossetti's most exquisite portrait of Miss Siddal, represents the end of the Dantesque phase in his work—a phase which had produced the translation of the early poets and such superb art as "Dante's Dream" (1856 and 1871).

Soon to Gabriel's love the darker shadows of actuality appear, and these intrude perhaps for the first time into the brilliance of the love ideal. As Doughty[6] suggests, Gabriel in his sonnet "Broken Music" records an early frustration—". . . the pang of unpermitted prayer"—that probably arose from the division of feeling between the two, Rossetti desiring Lizzie, and she demanding marriage; and probably also derived from Rossetti's own confusion in his interpretation of her, as woman or as concept. Additional anguish came with the early signs of Lizzie's failing health. However, Gabriel had discovered to his pleasure an artistic ability in Lizzie; and she, under his direction, began to sketch and paint, and soon to write poems that are largely statements of melancholy and self-pity.

In May, 1854, shortly before his father's death, Rossetti had taken Lizzie to Hastings for rest; by this time, she was becoming a permanent invalid. They remained in Hastings through July; while Lizzie worked on sketches for a book of Scottish ballads to be edited by William Allingham, Gabriel often succumbed to spells of indolence and futility, moods that were becoming more prevalent in his life. He became increasingly concerned over her health and more convinced of the possibility of her death; but Lizzie was also exerting pressure on Rossetti about marriage, a matter he grew more hesitant to consider. Lizzie's declining health and her growing insistence on marriage began doubtlessly to clash, in their inescapable harsh reality, with Gabriel's vision of ideal love. Such poems of this period as "Lost on Both Sides" (July 22, 1854) reflect growing disillusionment:

> . . . separate hopes, which in a soul had wooed
> The one same Peace, strove with each other long,
> And Peace before their faces perished since:
> So, through that soul, in restless brotherhood,
> They roam together now, and wind among
> Its bye-streets, knocking at the dusty inns.

The ideal and the actual, seeking a common unity in a single vision within the soul, find only awesome strife and division; and Peace perishes. In the last sonnet of his *House of Life* sequence Rossetti, in 1870, was again to plead for the vision, "the one Hope's one name"; and he hoped that after death Peace would not "be still a sunk stream long unmet."

In April, 1854, John Ruskin, who had seen and praised some of Rossetti's water colors and oils, met Gabriel, beginning a trouble-plagued friendship that was to end in anger and embittered feelings in July, 1865. In the autumn of 1854, Ruskin asked Gabriel to teach drawing at the Working Men's College, to which he agreed; for he was eager to please the wealthy critic, who, Rossetti reported to Ford Madox Brown, seemed "in a mood to make my fortune." In March, 1855, the friendship between the two men began to show results; Ruskin, wishing to alleviate some of the financial concerns for Gabriel and Lizzie, agreed to pay her a hundred and fifty pounds a year for her paintings. But Ruskin was soon to learn that his beneficence did not clear the way for Rossetti to set to work in earnest, a reason for Ruskin's financial assistance. Instead, Ruskin's funds encouraged indolence and distraction; and Lizzie, now financially independent, began to demand marriage; quarrels became common between her and Gabriel. In spring, 1856, Gabriel's "Woodspurge" was indicative of the growing strife and grief between the two lovers.

Earlier, in September, 1855, Ruskin, fearing the mounting turmoil he found between Lizzie and Gabriel, encouraged her to travel. Soon bankrupt in Paris, she urgently wrote Gabriel for funds; and he joined her there for a short time. Antipathy grew between Rossetti and Ruskin; for Gabriel pressed him for money, increasingly neglected Ruskin's critical suggestions, and faltered in his promised work. When Lizzie returned to England in the spring, 1856, her health had declined but her demands for marriage to Gabriel increased.

During these years of heightened anguish and frustration between Gabriel and Lizzie, until their marriage in May, 1860—a period of disappointment that doubtlessly challenged the Dantesque ideal of love—Rossetti still responded at times to his vision. His poem "The Birth-bond" (1854) recaptures the old idealism; lovers' souls, like twins, share a common sympathy: ". . . among souls allied to mine was yet/One nearer kindred. . . ." And in "Sudden Light" (1854) there is a foreshadowing of his later "The One Hope"; shall not time restore, after death, the beloved, and they become one? This poem echoes the younger Gabriel's vision and hope in "The Blessed Damozel."

By 1854 the Brotherhood, weakened considerably by dissension among the members, was falling apart. Hunt left for Palestine, not to return until 1856; Millais attacked Ruskin; Rossetti quarreled with Hunt; and all were angry with Rossetti because of his growing popularity and his increasing significance as leader of the group. Yet, at the same time that old alliances melted away, new ones were formed with young Oxford followers of Rossetti: Edward Burne-Jones and William Morris, both in 1856 undergraduates of Exeter College. Later to this group of admirers came Algernon Swinburne.

It was out of this new group of disciples that came an event of significant consequence to Rossetti. In the spring, 1857, Lizzie, still pressing for marriage and angry, went to visit relatives at Sheffield. Rossetti then went to Oxford, on his "Jovial Campaign," to paint the famous and now lost frescoes on the ten bays in the walls of Union Society Debating Hall. With him went Jones and Morris, as well as Val Prinsep, Roddam Stanhope, John Pollen, and Arthur Hughes. The designs the group selected were themes from Malory's *Morte d'Arthur.* Unfortunately, like a great many undertakings in Rossetti's life, this endeavor at Oxford was finally unrealized. A number of important factors contributed to this unsuccessful "campaign": lack of proper preparation of the walls to receive the paint, Rossetti's own desultory and uninterested efforts, and the holiday atmosphere that predominated among them.

Rossetti, as leader of this group, influenced the thought and writings of the younger men. Morris, beginning to write poetry at this time, had Gabriel's criticism in preparing some of his verses for publication; and the early poems of Swinburne also reveal the impact of Rossetti's work. Within this circle of emerging artists were appearing the first early indications of the esthetic movement that was to dominate the end of the century.

Jane Burden, soon to marry William Morris, was Rossetti's model for Guinevere in his painting for the Union Hall, a fresco that was to depict Sir Lancelot before the chapel of the San Grail. Rossetti described it as Lancelot "prevented by his sin from entering the chapel. . . . He has fallen asleep before the shrine full of angels, and, between him and it, rises in his dream the image of Queen Guinevere. . . ." The earlier studies of Guinevere made by Dante Gabriel were from Lizzie, but later studies and the painting are from Janey. Both Doughty[7] and Mégroz[8] record that Gabriel probably persuaded Morris to marry the "stunner" to keep her in the group. Later rumors indicated that Dante Gabriel had fallen in love with Janey himself but that the tie with Lizzie remained.

Other women were to play a role in Rossetti's life, women whose attraction contrasted to the sickly, pursuing Lizzie. She had returned to England in 1856 to find Dante Gabriel attentive to Hunt's model, Annie Miller; Lizzie in her growing anger broke off that relationship; but others developed, as with Fanny Cornforth, who, appearing in his oil "Bocca Baciata" (1859), became for Rossetti the original for many of his later sensuous female portraits. Janey Morris was to emerge later, after 1867, as a primary influence on Rossetti's life and work. Their meeting at Oxford, during the "Campaign" was an eventful one for Gabriel; for him Janey was to become a possible fulfillment of his vision, one questionably fulfilled by Lizzie. But the ties with Lizzie remained a while longer. In November, 1857, after his long absence at Oxford, Dante Gabriel was called away; Lizzie was ill. In April, 1859, Morris and Jane Burden were married at Oxford.

IV *The Dantesque Ideal Ebbs*

During the late 1859 and early 1860 period, Rossetti was making a significant change in his art. In the autumn of 1859 Gabriel finished the "Bocca Baciata" painting of Fanny, his first important work in oil since his "Ecce Ancilla Domini" (1850). Holman Hunt remarked that at this time Rossetti's work on the Llandaff triptych —the Cardiff Cathedral altarpiece commissioned in 1855 and finally completed in 1864—was executed at the "turning point of his life . . . from his [Rossetti's] first severity of style to a more sensuous manner." [9] From his subjects found in *Morte d'Arthur,* such as his "Sir Galahad Receiving the Grail" (1857) and "Sir Galahad at the Shrine" (1859), and from Dante themes, such as "The Salutation of Beatrice" (1859), Rossetti turned more and more to the physical.

The suggestion that his ascetic idol yet haunted him and a clue perhaps to his emotional reactions at the time of his marriage to Lizzie in May, 1860, are found in the pen and ink sketch, "How They Met Themselves." Drawn during Gabriel and Lizzie's honeymoon in Paris, the sketch presents the *doppelganger* theme: two lovers lost in a woods are faced with their own apparitions. His dissatisfaction with whatever escape to the physical he may have found in such women as Fanny Cornforth, and his continued disillusionment in the fading image of his ideal, projected in Lizzie, may be sensed in the poetry he was writing in the last months before his marriage. "A Little While," like "A New-Year's Burden," echoes with the melancholy of love now being terminated and with the end of the hoped-for vision in which love is elevated:

A little while a little love
  The hour yet bears for thee and me
  Who have not drawn the veil to see
If still our heaven be lit above.

. . . .

The branches cross above our eyes,
  The skies are in a net:
And what's the thing beneath the skies
  We two would most forget?
  . . . .

The love once ours, but ours long hours ago.

Doughty suggests[10] that Rossetti's poem "The Song of the Bower" of early 1860, written before Dante Gabriel's marriage, indicates the poet's attitude toward Lizzie, his sense of evil omen in the coming event, and his separation from more desirable women. The poem does end with a suggestion of the "One Hope" of 1870: ". . . at what goal may we meet?" Swinburne believed the poem referred not to Lizzie, as William Rossetti was to state in his *Memoir,*[11] but to Fanny Cornforth. In any event, the poem does, at this date, reflect a concept of love idealized by separation. In all probability Rossetti had transferred, to some degree, the vision to Fanny. Although Fanny was doubtlessly never a suitable counterpart to that ideal, she was merely for Gabriel at the time a resolution of his dilemma; he needed from her the physical gratification that he obviously was not discovering in the failing Lizzie.

Lizzie gave birth to a dead child in May, 1861; and her earlier brooding mood, dispelled for a while after her marriage, returned. It was also in 1861 that Gabriel published his earlier Italian poets translations, *The Early Italian Poets;* in this volume appeared his translation of Dante's *Vita Nuova.* Ironically, at the very time of this publication, culminating long work by Gabriel on Dante and his contemporaries, the Dantesque ideal was ebbing away. Lizzie's simple verse of the period reflects her own disappointed love and her growing concern with death:

And, mother, when the big tears fall,
  (And fall, God knows they may),
Tell him I died of my great love,
  And my dying heart was gay.

On February 11, 1862, Lizzie died from an overdose of laudanum, a drug she had used frequently during the last year to combat sleeplessness. The circumstances of her death remain vague; for, though the inquest on February 12 established the point that the large overdose was accidental, those close to Rossetti hinted at suicide. On the evening of February 10, Lizzie, Gabriel, and Swinburne had dined together in Leicester Square. At eight o'clock the Rossettis went home; and later, when Gabriel left the house, Lizzie was preparing to retire. Returning at eleven-thirty, he found her unconscious and the room reeking of laudanum. Oscar Wilde in later years reported that Gabriel, angry with Lizzie on their return home, asserted, when she asked for more laudanum, "There, take the lot!" and then thrust the bottle into her hands. Whatever the facts of Lizzie's death, the actual circumstances surrounding the event seem to have plagued Rossetti in the years following.

The grief-stricken Gabriel, unobserved, placed in Lizzie's coffin the only manuscript copy he had of poems he had been preparing for a volume. It was this manuscript that Rossetti authorized to be reclaimed from his wife's grave in 1869 when the poetic inspiration once again returned and he entertained hopes of publication. The profoundness of Gabriel's feelings for the dead Lizzie were to be caught in his painting of 1863, "Beata Beatrix." Mégroz's comment on this work is interesting:[12] ". . . that picture is less a man's memorial to a frail and lovely creature who needed his protection, than the aspiring prayer of a childlike and yet beautiful soul to an ideal removed to desperate distances by the death of a loved person." Mégroz calls "Beata Beatrix" the "culmination of Rossetti's peculiar idealism."

In October, 1862, Gabriel moved to 16 Cheyne Walk, Chelsea, which was to be his home for the remaining years, years so often marked with regret and anguish, as seen in his sonnet "Lost Days." Fanny Cornforth became a companion often in these days in which he pursued his new interest in what Bell Scott was to call pictures of "women and flowers." Marillier[13] speaks of this period when Rossetti turned to single-figure subjects, "lavishing upon them indeed all the wealth of his fine imagination, and surrounding them with quaint and beautiful accessories. . . . Many of these accessories, picked up during his rambles among the curiosity shops. . . ." The first oils of this type were "Fazio's Mistress"

(1863), "Lady Lilith" (1864), "Venus Verticordia" (1864), and "Monna Vanna" (1866). These portraits, representing so much the vibrancy and attraction of physical beauty, became an antipodal counterpart to so much of Rossetti's early work depicting Dantesque and medieval themes, pictures that Lizzie had figured in so often. Rossetti labored industriously in the first years following Lizzie's death in an attempt to control his growing debts. These became years of growing popularity, with new commissions and new buyers.

But in late 1866 there was a beginning decline in his health, brought on by overwork and by a strenuous life of dissipation with new mistresses. Later, hydrocele developed, requiring medical attention. In 1867 insomnia began to plague Dante Gabriel and did so for the rest of his life. Such later poems as "Sleepless Dreams" (1868), "A Superscription" (1868), and "Soul's Sphere" (1873) reveal the nightmare of sleeplessness. With insomnia came a new fear of failing eyesight, a fear enlarged by Rossetti's memory of his father's blindness. In September, 1868, unable to paint, he visited Penkill Castle, Ayrshire, the estate of Miss Alice Boyd. It was in this period of illness that Rossetti surprisingly began to write poetry in earnest again. Interestingly, too, it was at this time that Janey Morris returned to play an increasingly significant role in Gabriel's life.

Since 1866 the Morrises had lived in London, primarily because of the demands upon William Morris of his "firm," organized in 1861 by Morris, Marshall, Faulkner, Webb, Rossetti, Brown, and Jones. The intention of the firm was to revive the decorative arts and to enable people of taste to secure beautiful pieces of furniture and decoration. The industry of Morris helped the firm to succeed, and it became Morris' chief concern in his life. In 1866 Rossetti began the famous oil of Janey, seated at a table with a glass of roses; it was completed in 1868. In 1868 he began his "La Pia" from her, and completed the exquisite crayon drawings of her as "Aurea Catena" and "Reverie." Marillier remarks, concerning the many sketches of Janey Morris at this time, that these permitted Rossetti to build up "materials for much of his subsequent work, just as he had previously done in the case of Miss Siddal." [14]

The love poems written during 1869–1870 reveal the new rapture Rossetti discovered in the reawakened feeling for Mrs. Morris, a reaction amply discussed and supported by Doughty in his biography of Rossetti. If the fact can be accepted that these enraptured statements of love in the sonnets of this period are commemorative of Gabriel's love for Janey and are not poems of tribute to the memory of the dead Lizzie, then Mrs. Morris became the personification of his shaken ideal, the union of both the physical and spiritual facets of his love vision. The same language of religious ritual that Rossetti would have found in Keats' "Eve of St. Agnes" [15]—in which the adoration of, longing for, and experience in the most profound of physical love are transmuted to the higher spiritual form:

> ". . . Ah, silver shrine, here will I take my rest
> After so many hours of toil and quest,
> A famish'd pilgrim,—sav'd by miracle. . . ."

—is found in Rossetti's "Love's Testament" (1869):

> O thou who at Love's hour ecstatically
> Unto my heart dost evermore present,
> Clothed with his fire, thy heart his testament;
> Whom I have neared and felt thy breath to be
> The inmost incense of his sanctuary.

In 1864 Rossetti was entertaining thoughts of publishing a volume of original poetry, but his only manuscripts of earlier poems lay with Lizzie in her grave. Not until the 1868 reawakening of poetic inspiration did he begin to feel he had possibly enough verse for this contemplated book. Many of Gabriel's close friends, Scott, Swinburne, Morris, and Meredith, had published their poetry, as had Christina, his sister, in 1862 with her *Goblin Market* volume, and in 1866 with her *Prince's Progress.* He had, in his *Early Italian Poets* of 1861, promised such a book. Friends had encouraged him to retrieve the buried manuscript; and Dante Gabriel, in August, 1869, authorized their recovery from Lizzie's grave. He left for a vacation at Penkill Castle, Ayrshire, hoping the exhumation would be completed in his absence. Gabriel, in an attempt at salving conscience, half convinced himself that Lizzie would have had it so.

After much delay, the manuscript was secured and passed back to Rossetti. When *Poems* appeared in late April, 1870, the volume established Rossetti as a successful poet-artist. Long deeply sensitive of public reaction to his work, having sworn never to exhibit publicly his art again after the attacks in 1850 on his "Ecce Ancilla Domini," Gabriel had worked hard and carefully to ensure favorable criticism of *Poems*. He secured the help of close friends in reviewing his volume in the various important critical journals; but Swinburne's praise in the *Fortnightly*, a well-known panegyric, embarrassed Rossetti: ". . . full of splendid things of course, but too much so in all reason." Some few unfavorable criticisms appeared; the unsigned article in *Blackwood's* was rumored to be the work of a personal friend. By 1870 Rossetti's sense of a conspiracy against him had developed, a grim mental quirk that was to increase in intensity as Rossetti grew older.

A month before the publication of *Poems*, Rossetti had gone to Scalands, the country home of Madame Bodichon, for a rest, accompanied by William Stillman, an American journalist. Gabriel and Lizzie had visited Scalands sixteen years before; and, on this return visit, he recalled many memories of her. When insomnia and weakened eyesight troubled him increasingly, Stillman suggested chloral as a remedy for Rossetti's sleeplessness, a drug that was to have a disastrous effect on Rossetti. William Rossetti records the result:[16] "constant insomnia (beginning towards 1867), and its counteraction by reckless drugging with chloral, cooperated, no doubt, to the same disastrous end [the gravely altered tone of Rossetti's mind and character] . . . in making my brother a changed man from 1872 onwards." William believed that the evil effects of chloral, plus the damaging impact of Buchanan's "Fleshly School" article in 1871, caused the ultimate degeneration of his brother.

The abusive critical review by Robert Buchanan appeared in the *Contemporary Review* of October, 1871. The charge of "fleshliness" against any art form was indeed a severe one with deep-rooted cultural significance in England in 1871, but the presence and awareness of the human body, as well as of its animalistic emotions, are in Rossetti's verse. In his attraction to such women as Fanny Cornforth, representative of the most basic erotic sensations, Gabriel was contributing disastrously to the very division between the flesh and the spirit that his dream endeavored to unite. In an attempt to rejoin these two worlds Rossetti tried to express the physical in the heightened terms of the "Love's Testament" sonnet. This direct handling of physical sensations Buchanan, using the pseudonym "Thomas Maitland," ferreted out in phrases and lines scattered throughout Rossetti's verse; and these he used for his attack.

The effects of this article upon Rossetti were indeed profound. William, writing in 1881, spoke of the impact on his brother: ". . . he allowed a sense of unfair treatment, and a suspicion that the slur cast upon himself and his writings might be widely accepted as true, to eat into his very vitals, gravely altering his tone of mind and character, his attitude towards the world, and his habits of life." [17] Gabriel later in a composed, efficient manner replied in "The Stealthy School of Criticism," which appeared in *Athenaeum* of December, 1871. And, in spite of the revelation of Buchanan's identity in May, 1872, Buchanan repeated his abuse by reprinting his article in pamphlet form.

At this time, Gabriel's weakened condition—the result of overwork, insomnia, fear of blindness, chloral—and his growing hypersensitivity made him a particularly vulnerable target. As William asserted, the tone of his mind was gravely altered; and he had become increasingly distressed, withdrawn, and suspicious. Even Browning, long an idol to Gabriel and more recently a personal friend, came under Rossetti's demented suspicions. Finally in June, 1872, the crisis came when Gabriel received a copy of Browning's "Fifine at the Fair" and found in it what he thought were direct allusions and insults to him. Even Lewis Carroll's "Hunting of the Snark" was found, like "Fifine," to be a source of ridicule to him. Around June 2, according to Scott and William, Gabriel temporarily lost sanity, betraying him, as William recorded,[18] "into the belief that he was fast becoming the object of widespread calumny and obloquy. . . ."

Dr. Gordon Hake, a friend, took Rossetti into his own house at Roehampton. During the second night at Hake's, June 3, haunted by delusions and accusing voices, Rossetti, attempting suicide, swallowed a phial of laudanum. His deep coma was mistaken for sleep, and not until late the next day did William learn of the attempt; but he never told his mother or sisters the circumstances behind Dante Gabriel's illness. For half a year Rossetti suffered, as a result, partial paralysis of the hip. At the end of September, after partial recovery, he traveled to Kelmscott Manor, the old

Elizabethan house leased in May, 1871, by Morris and him. Janey Morris and her children were there.

In July of the year before, Gabriel had stayed at Kelmscott with Janey. Earlier in that month William Morris had left England for Iceland because of his interest in the sagas. During those happy days Dante Gabriel painted Mrs. Morris as "Water-Willow." By mid-August on that first visit he had written thirty new love sonnets for his *House of Life* and had also completed the ballad "Rose Mary." In early October he had learned of the Buchanan article and had returned to London to read the article for himself.

When Rossetti returned, after the crisis of June, to Kelmscott Manor in September, 1872, he told William, "Here all is happiness again . . . ."; and he remained there two years. He began painting Janey again as "Proserpine," an oil that gave him much trouble, necessitating many studies and seven attempts on canvas before it was completed in 1873. The beautiful Alexa Wilding came in the spring of 1873 to sit for Gabriel's oil "La Ghirlandata." Gabriel prepared a second edition of *Early Italian Poets,* renamed it *Dante and His Circle,* and changed the dedication from Lizzie to his mother; the volume appeared in December.

V *Years of Slow Decline*

Most of the poems Rossetti wrote during 1873 are sonnets that appear in his *House of Life;* they reveal fairly clearly the state of Rossetti's mind during this second stay at Kelmscott. Such sonnets as "The Soul's Sphere," "The Heart of Night," "The Sun's Shame, II," and "Life the Beloved" indicate the obsessive, morbid mental reflections of such earlier poems as "Lost on Both Sides" (1854) and "Known in Vain" (1853). By the spring of 1874, decided signs of decline in his physical and mental health were noticeable to many.

In July, the Morrises left England for a tour of Belgium; and Rossetti left Kelmscott, never to return, for he gave up his part tenancy of the manor at that time. Soon William Morris was actively assuming control of "The Firm," paying compensation to the various remaining members, and ejecting them. The breach which had been developing between Dante Gabriel and William Morris was completed; estrangement became final.

The years remaining were ones of slow decline for Rossetti,

with but infrequent trips away from the brooding atmosphere of 16 Cheyne Walk. As the delusion of a widespread conspiracy against him grew, it was abetted by more crises with chloral and increased problems with debts. But, in the solitude of the house at Cheyne Walk, Rossetti began working hard. In 1875 he produced the painting "La Bella Mano," an oil in which critics began to see signs of the artist's decline. In these last years of Gabriel's life, there were many indications that his powerful color sense had begun to deteriorate; moreover, the exaggeration in his portrayal of necks and lips appeared more and more frequently. These indications of failings and distortion in his conception and execution were doubtlessly results of his growing morbidity.

Unfortunately, when these last large important portraits of women by Rossetti became known, the public mistakenly construed what they saw to be the Rossetti style; it did not know that these paintings were but a small portion of his work, most of which is free of these signs of deterioration of power. "La Bella Mano" is the first oil that signals clearly the beginning of this last period and the close of the earlier one of pictures of a more exalted range of conception, such as "Lilith," "Beata Beatrix," "Sibylla Palmifera," and "La Ghirlandata."

Along with George Hake, Rossetti went to Aldwick Lodge, Bognor, Sussex, in October, 1875, following a period of overwork, insomnia, and worry over increasing debts. For nine months Gabriel spent what Theodore Watts-Dunton called "the most secluded life he ever led." His deep-seated morbidity and dejection continued through this period at Bognor, and his consumption of chloral reached a dangerous point. When his health began deteriorating quickly in April, 1876, Gabriel wrote out instructions concerning his death, perhaps believing he was dying; he forbade burial at Highgate, where Lizzie had been buried.

In his artistic work, inspiration was also ebbing. The melancholy and the anguished expression of his few 1873 poems are found in "The Trees of the Garden," in which he probes the dark inscrutable nature of fate and finds no answer:

> . . . is it all a show,—
> A wisp that laughs upon the wall?—decree
> Of some inexorable supremacy
> Which ever, as man strains his blind surmise

. . . looks past his eyes,
Sphinx-faced. . . .

In this same year Rossetti completed "The Question" or "The Sphinx," a large pencil drawing depicting a monster, emblem of the mystery of life and death, seated, blindly gazing into space. Three figures approach, representing youth, manhood, and old age; and all are determined to draw from the silent form an answer to questions most important to them. Rossetti was prompted to do this sketch following the untimely death of Ford Madox Brown's brilliant son, Oliver, a young man for whom Rossetti had much admiration. For Dante Gabriel, Death and the unknowable darkness of life itself came forth as primary concerns. His poem "Hero's Lamp" (1875) links the two great polarities of his thought, Life and Death: "Lo where Love walks, Death's pallid neophyte." The gloom of his personal concerns in "A Superscription" (1868)—"Look in my face; my name is Might-have-been;/I am also called No-more, Too-late, Farewell . . ."—now spread to encompass his vision of total life, of all men's Fate. This mood continues in 1876 in "Adieu":

Sinking suffering heart
That know'st how weary thou art,—
Soul so fain for a flight,—
Aye, spread your wings to depart,
Sad soul and sorrowing heart,—
Adieu, Farewell, Good-night.

Interestingly enough, in this period of depression and poor health (1876), while visiting Broadlands, the home of the Cowper-Temples, Rossetti worked on his painting "The Blessed Damozel," that had been commissioned in 1873 by William Graham. The oil was to be an attempt to realize on canvas the intensity of the poem of Gabriel's youth. In 1872 he had done a crayon study for the oil. In December, 1877, a predella was commissioned to be added to the main picture. In 1879, introducing some important changes, Rossetti painted a replica of this oil for F. R. Leyland.

Serious illness came again in May, 1877; and in mid-August, when Gabriel was ordered to leave London for his health, he stayed at Herne Bay near Margate for two months, struggling with a drastic reduction in his chloral consumption which his doctor had required. In mid-November Mrs. Morris was going abroad, and this fact brought Rossetti back to London to see her leave for Italy, where she remained until the summer of 1878, seemingly withdrawn from her more familiar relationship with Gabriel. When increased debts drove him more to painting replicas, his creative power dimmed because of this recourse to potboiling, and his ideals faded, including the vision of ideal love.

The large oil "Salutation of Beatrice," which he began in 1880, was not a successful picture. Despite the vibrant source that the Dante themes had earlier been, especially the significance of the Beatrice figure, this unfinished painting displays all the defects of his later style. These same late period modifications in his painting appear also in the oil "La Donna della Finestra," 1879. This subject had been in Rossetti's mind from earlier years when he had handled so often the Dantesque themes. From the *Vita Nuova,* this picture concerns the lady seen by Dante, who, when overcome by his grief at the death of Beatrice, saw her looking down upon him. Dante, as Gabriel translated the work, says of her: "the very sum of pity appeared gathered together in her."

The head for this oil was sketched from Mrs. Morris, but Rossetti introduced the morbid characteristics of his late style into the depiction. Gabriel believed that this woman, "The Lady of Pity," might be Gemma Donati, whom Dante later married. William Rossetti, in discussing this lady from the *Vita Nuova,* remarks:[19]

> Humanly she is the Lady at the Window; mentally she is the Lady of Pity. This interpenetration of soul and body . . . this externalism and internalism—are constantly to be understood as the key-note of Rossetti's aim and performance in art. I have emphasized the point here, as the particular subject from the *Vita Nuova,* with its dubious balance . . . between the actual and allegorical. . . . but remarks to the like effect might . . . apply to the general range and scope of his [Rossetti's] art from first to last.

This comment by William speaks to the double vision of love which Rossetti early held and his attempt to fuse the two through his intensity of statement. We are tempted, in tracing so many parallels between Rossetti and the Dante of *Vita Nuova,* to wonder about Rossetti's handling of Dante's Lady of Pity. Especially we question his use of Janey Morris as model and his modifications of her features. Marillier,[20] in commenting about these defects of style, attributes them to a "growing morbidity of temperament." Perhaps these characteristics are external projections, as William states, of an internal recognition of the failure of a dream and are an actual allegory in style of disillusionment. The "Lady of Pity" was left uncompleted by Rossetti.

During most of 1880, Rossetti surprisingly enjoyed a return of improved mental and physical health. A renewed interest in poetry found Gabriel busy with ballad and narrative verse; the historical ballad "The White Ship" was completed in 1880. The spring of 1881 found him hard at work on a new volume, *Ballads and Sonnets.* The long ballad "The King's Tragedy" was finished then; and Rossetti compiled, in the present sequence, the *House of Life* sonnets to publish them with the ballads. At this same time Rossetti wished to reissue an edition of his earlier *Poems* of 1870, which was out of print by 1881; but, with the transfer of the *House of Life* sonnets to the new *Ballads and Sonnets,* he had to find material to take their place in the edition. This he did with the unfinished narrative poem "The Bride's Prelude." To the two ballads "The White Ship" and "The King's Tragedy" Rossetti wished to add a third ballad on Joan of Arc, but it was not begun. Both volumes were published in mid-September.

The sonnets of these last years are unlike most of the earlier verse he wrote, for they are primarily academic in nature. After rereading the works of such Romantics as Blake, Shelley, Keats, Chatterton, and Coleridge—in preparation to assist Mrs. Alexander Gilchrist in a second edition of her husband's *Life of Blake*—Rossetti wrote a poem on each of these figures. Of Keats, he wrote: "Weary with labour spurned and love found vain,/In dead Rome's sheltering shadow wrapped his sleep"; and of Chatterton: "thy grave unknown/And love-dream of thine unrecorded face."

As may be seen from these quotations, Rossetti projected in these late commemorative sonnets his own frustrations and his anger with a fate that dismayed his sensitive spirit. These poems, impersonal in subject, speak of his own unhappiness about his decline, his failure, and his loss of visions and ideals. In 1880, in his poem "A Sonnet is a Moment's Monument," which introduces his *House of Life,* Rossetti may insist that such verse is a "Memorial from the Soul's eternity"; but few poems of these remaining years become so for him. In the 1880 sonnet "The Song Throe" he says much the same thing: verse is primarily self-expression. Nonetheless, the sonnet, "Day-Dream," written for the oil he completed this same year of Mrs. Morris, mentions woman, but not in the earlier more arduous and idealistic terms.

As the 1880's began, a new group of poets and writers came forward as the new figures in the esthetic movement; they regarded Rossetti as a leader. Ironically, Gabriel had little sympathy for these "esthetes" and their increasingly extreme art. But into the loneliness of his last years came Hall Caine, the young clerk from Liverpool, who had literary ambitions of his own. Caine records his full story of his late association with Rossetti in his *Recollections.* On his first visit in 1880 to Cheyne Walk, Gabriel showed him the beautiful canvas of Janey Morris, "The Day-Dream." And Caine wrote: "I cannot forget the pallid face of the painter as he stood beside it, or the close atmosphere of his studio, with its smell of paint and the musty odour of accumulated treasures lying long undisturbed. . . ." [21] In August, 1881, Caine moved into Cheyne Walk as a companion to Rossetti.

During the spring and summer of 1881, Rossetti's health once again drastically declined; there was another chloral crisis. In September, convinced that a change of scene was necessary, he set off, accompanied by Caine and Fanny Cornforth, for the English Lakes. Financial needs necessitated his resuming painting, mostly replicas; but one bit of good fortune occurred: the sale of his original large oil "Dante's Dream." Painted earlier in 1870–1871 for William Graham, but resold a few years later to Mr. Valpy, because both owners were dissatisfied with the large size of the canvas, the oil came back to Rossetti in 1878 with whom it remained until its final sale to the Liverpool municipality in 1881. The news of this sale reached Rossetti just before his departure to the Lakes, where, in growing melancholy and sickness, he was to remain a month.

On October 17, Rossetti left the Lakes with Caine for London. The return trip from Cumberland, as Caine recounts it in his *Recollections,* was the occasion when Dante Gabriel, in despondency, revealed the secret of his love for Janey Morris. Caine portrays Gabriel as ". . . the figure of a man who, after engaging himself to one woman in all honour and good faith, had fallen in love with another, and then gone on to marry the first out of a mistaken sense of loyalty. . . ." [22]

When Gabriel entered Cheyne Walk again, he exclaimed, as he entered the door, that he would never leave his home again. His illness continued; his old hallucinations increased; and his fears grew of conspiracies against him, of coming blindness, of growing debts, and, ultimately, of death itself. His old visionary ideal of the "One Hope" when the "wan soul . . ./Peers breathless for the gift of grace" seemed little consolation. On December 11, 1881, he suffered paralysis of the left side, a result of the chloral; and on December 19 the drug was banished, never to be resumed. For a while in January, 1882, he improved enough to complete a duplicate oil of "Joan of Arc" for Mr. Valpy; but his left arm and hand remained paralyzed.

Once again Rossetti was encouraged to leave London; and in February he traveled with Hall Caine, Caine's young sister, and a nurse to Birchington-on-Sea, where an old friend, John Seddon, offered Gabriel the use of his bungalow. William Rossetti records[23] that his brother, perhaps as early as 1847, wrote part of a comic ballad on Jan van Hunks, the story of a Dutchman who, in a smoking match with the Devil, lost his soul to that fiend. During his last days at Birchington-on-Sea, despite his steadily failing health, Rossetti completed this comic poem by the end of March, 1882, just a few days before his death. In April he unsuccessfully attempted to complete his unfinished youthful tale "St. Agnes of Intercession." On April 5 he dictated to Hall Caine two sonnets on his pencil sketch "The Sphinx," the last verses he composed. On Easter Day, April 9, 1882, Rossetti died; and he was buried in the churchyard of Birchington-on-Sea on April 14. Christina Rossetti's sonnet "Birchington Churchyard" caught the mood of the place:

> A lowly hill which overlooks a flat,
> Half sea, half country-side;
> A flat-shored sea of low-voiced creeping tide
> Over a chalky weedy mat.

CHAPTER 3

Translations and Prose

ROSSETTI'S dream has its roots in the early years, particularly 1845–1849. In this short period of his youth the vision takes shape, drawing its form from diverse sources: from early readings, imbued with a sense of the adventurous, supernatural, and romantic; and particularly from the contact with early Italian poets and with Dante. Rossetti's father, Gabriele, wrote with pleasure to his friend Charles Lyell in 1836, "Gabriel Charles Dante is continually reading; this is his first passion, his second is for drawing. He knows many passages of Shakespeare by heart, and recites them energetically. He devours a book with more appetite, and perhaps more quickly, than I do." [1]

I *Early Influences*

William Rossetti, in his later writings, has also attested to the wide, varied reading of the young Gabriel. His earliest enthusiasm was for Shakespeare. His fascination with an illustrated translation of *Faust* and his interest in Scott, Ariosto, *The Arabian Nights,* and later Byron indicate where much of the youthful Dante Gabriel's curiosity lay—the Gothic, macabre, mysterious, and supernatural. *Tales of Chivalry, Gil Blas, Don Quixote, The Newgate Calendar,* and *Legends of Terror* were read along with Dickens. In 1844 Shelley replaced Rossetti's excitement over Byron, followed by Keats; and after 1844, came Dumas, Poe, Coleridge, Blake, and others.

Not until about sixteen did Gabriel read Dante for himself, despite the omnipresence of the Italian poet in the house. For Dante Gabriel and for his brother and sisters, the sight of the old Gabriele, surrounded by the stacks of books on alchemy, Swedenborg, freemasonry, and mysticism, was a source of awe; but his voluminous, esoteric studies of Dante were for sometime representative of dullness. Nonetheless, the presence of such strange materials influenced the children and contributed immensely to the love of the preternatural and weird of Gabriel. But, among a myriad of writers, Dante became primary, contributing significantly, along with the Gothic, to Rossetti's later work in verse and painting. As Waller remarks in his study of the early years,[2] "The fusion and confusion of these two elements [Dantesque and Gothic] in his mind gives the key to almost all of his work."

At six, Rossetti had written "The Slave," a dramatic poem with obvious Shakespearean overtones. At the same time the youngster was sketching subjects from the Shakespeare plays and gathering what he considered "Beauties of Shakespeare," passages that attracted his vibrant imagination. The first composition following "The Slave" was written in 1840, when Rossetti, then twelve, was influenced by chivalric romance to write "Roderick and Rosalba, a Story of the Round Table." The atmosphere of the Morte d'Arthur world was to affect many of Rossetti's drawings and to stimulate the work of the "Jovial Campaign" at the Oxford Union Hall in 1857. In 1843, Grandfather Polidori printed on his private press Gabriel's poem "Sir Hugh the Heron," a juvenile piece that Dante Gabriel later was afraid might someday be "foisted" into public print. This tale, like so much of his early writing, deals with the world of chivalry, love, and rescues; and it indicates the strange mixture of Dante and Arthur that colors so much of Rossetti's thought: a "lady bright" named Beatrice is rescued by Sir Hugh from a pirate band. Interspersed with the action of this tale are also early signs of Rossetti's infatuation with the magical and the otherworldly. The influence of German romance produced, at fifteen, a short ballad "William and Marie," which also deals with knights and fair ladies. The prose tale "Sorrentino," written at about this same time, introduces, from the German literature, the Devil as a character—an interest later manifested in the pen-and-ink sketches of 1848, "Gretchen and Mephistopheles in the Chapel" and "Retro Me Sathana." It was also in this period that Rossetti began his grotesque ballad "Jan van Hunks" about the Devil and a boastful Dutchman.

At this time, when Gabriel was writing these juvenile pieces, all romantic and medieval, and involving an interest in the supernatural that he was always to have, he began his translations. G. A. Burger's "Lenore" was translated about 1844. William records[3] that his brother also worked with the opening chaunts of the twelfth-century German epic *Nibelungenlied*, Hartmann von Aue's *Arme Heinrich*, and a ballad from Prosper Mérimée's tale, *Colomba*. The work on these pieces, while Gabriel was yet in his teens, served as his apprenticeship as a translator.

Again, in a letter to Lyell on October 27, 1848, Gabriele speaks of his son's writings, saying that on that day Dante Gabriel had finished his translation of Dante's *La Vita Nuova*. We are told that in November, 1850, Rossetti was "translating *canzoni* at a great rate of evenings." [4] These translations not only played an important part in the formation of Rossetti's own style but also contributed significantly to his understanding of Dante. Gabriel commented that he had to find out everything for himself, but that he believed the translations worth doing, "as they are an immense accession even to one's means of understanding Dante's early life. . . ."

The care and fidelity that Rossetti brought to the translations of these works by Dante and his contemporaries are a result of his "understanding of Dante's early life" and of what he had himself brought to that work. As evidenced in his earlier, youthful work, and certainly as experienced in most of his later mature work, that "understanding" was an idealization of love, a vision that is heightened, nebulous, and romantic. The Dantesque symbols and ideas are assimilated into and colored by a Gothic environment. From Dante's *Vita Nuova*, Beatrice became for the young man a symbol of perfection, of idealized passion.

Mégroz[5] calls the *Vita Nuova* "the perfect expression of the sublime egoism of beauty-worshipping youth. With the intermediary symbol of the figure of love, his Lord, the poet really identifies the imperishable part of himself. Beatrice is a kind of self-realization, a necessary symbol of an exalted beauty." Rossetti himself says in his introduction to *Dante and His Circle* that the *Vita Nuova* "is a book which only youth could have produced, and which must chiefly remain sacred to the young." To the young, Rossetti continues, the figure of Beatrice is "less lifelike than lovelike . . . the friend of his own heart."

II *The Troubadour Poets*

From the verse found in Rossetti's volume of translations entitled *Early Italian Poets*, we find much that constitutes Rossetti's concept of love: the figure of the god of Love; the connection between the physical and the spiritual; the duality of love and death; and the desire to join the beloved after death. As stated earlier, Rossetti began these translations of the twelfth- to fourteenth-century Italian poets when he was but seventeen. The impact of these often highly sensitive and intensely emotional works on the young Rossetti can be traced in both style and idea throughout his work.

The idealization of love, that Rossetti found in these poets, began around 1100 in southern France; and it was soon spread throughout Europe by the troubadours, who represented love as a creed wherein man found his happiness in an exalted devotion to woman. For many fathers of the Catholic Church, the new romantic passion became a contradiction of the Christian moral order. And, significantly, in this century the Virgin became foremost in popular devotion and the subject of a vast literature of an amatory character. From this union of the religious and the secular and from the church's ultimate recognition of the idea that it was acceptable to love the beauty of God in woman emerged a reconciliation to be found in the love of Dante and Beatrice. What evolved finally was a kind of poetry that resembled allegory, wherein the beloved often connoted the Blessed Virgin. What began as songs of a young lover who sought the attention of a haughty lady became with Dante a mystical experience of profound depth and cosmological application. Rossetti found the full scope of this growth in the love concept through the verses he translated; and Dante's *Vita Nuova* appropriately becomes the final crystallization of that concept. But, unlike Dante, Rossetti never achieved the transformation to the higher vision.

The Early Italian Poets was printed with the financial help of John Ruskin; Gabriel dedicated the volume, "Whatever is mine in this book is inscribed to my wife. D. G. R., 1861." Critical judgments concerning Rossetti's handling of the translations have varied: William Sharp,[6] in an early study of Rossetti (1882), believes that "all are admirable"; Joseph Knight, in his *Life* (1887),[7] finds the collection a remarkable success; the chief criticism that Arthur Benson found, in his "English Men of Letters" study of Rossetti (1904), was that certain variations Rossetti introduced tended "to screw Dante's note up a little higher." [8] The first important study that attempts to look closely at the translations themselves is in R. L. Mégroz's book;[9] he examines a number of the poems to demonstrate that much of the ornate and involved characteristics of Rossetti's later style originated in his work with these early poets: long, tortured sentences; the use of "a mere filler to stop a vacancy"; and the awkward handling of rhymes.

R. D. Waller, in his *Rossetti Family* (1932), challenged Mégroz's conclusions, stating that he had based his assertions about Rossetti's inherited stylistic tendencies on a misreading of a letter from Rossetti to C. E. Norton in July, 1858. The original letter remarked that obscurities are "a thousand times more murky in the originals," and Mégroz reported Rossetti as writing that they are "a thousand times more murky *than* in the originals." Waller insists that, had Mégroz examined the original poems, he would have discovered that Rossetti was right. For Waller, the translations become "the finest tribute to Dante paid by the Rossetti family." [10]

In Rossetti's "Preface to the First Edition (1861)," he states what he considers to be his responsibility as translator: "The life-blood of rhythmical translation is this commandment,—that a good poem shall not be turned into a bad one. The only true motive for putting poetry into a fresh language must be to endow a fresh nation, as far as possible, with one more possession of beauty." To this commandment, as the majority of scholars are willing to admit, Rossetti was faithful.

It is profitable to examine a few of these early poets in chronological order, as Rossetti originally had them in his 1861 edition, to achieve a clearer understanding of the love concept. Ciullo d'Alcamo's "Dialogue, Lover and Lady," dated as 1172, appears first; and in it are signs of the early troubadour love poetry, but there is some debasement: the woman is haughty and militant, and the lover suffers from his rejected love. The man pursues, and the woman finally yields to his wish. The emphasis is on the physical aspects of love and nowhere is there reference to spiritual elevation.

In the second translation, from de' Folcachieri, dated 1177, "He speaks of His Condition Through Love," reference is made to Love, personified as a lord, who rules the lover:

> I know that it must certainly be Love:
> No other Lord, being thus set over me,
> Had judged me to this curse.

This use of personification influenced Dante, who elevates the significance of Love and argues in his *Vita Nuova* for such usage. Rossetti also adopts this use of personification from Dante and other early poets, especially in his *House of Life* sonnets.

The de' Folcachieri canzone is more within the spirit of the early troubadour poetry, for the lover suffers and wishes to serve his beloved in dedicated service. Rejection of lustful love is found in the poems of Guido Guinicelli, the poet Rossetti admired so much. In his famous canzone of 1220, "Of the Gentle Heart"—

> . . . evil natures meet
> With Love as it were water met with fire
> As cold abhorring heat.
> Through gentle heart Love doth a track divine,—
> Like knowing like. . . .

—appear the signs of the union of love and religious feeling to come. Interestingly, the peculiar relation between the physical and the spiritual that Rossetti reveals in his poetry is not totally absent in the verse of this early period. In the sonnet, "Of his Lady in Heaven," of 1250 by Jacopo da Lentino, there is a hint of Rossetti's own "The Blessed Damozel"; the lover wishes ultimately to enter Paradise, but only if he can do so in the company of his beloved:

> Without my lady I were loth to go,—
> She who has the bright face and the bright hair;
> Because if she were absent, I being there,
> My pleasure would be less than nought, I know.

The "bright hair," found in so much of this early verse, made an obvious impact on Rossetti's art and poetry.

But for da Lentino there is no hint of discovering in the beautiful lady the presence of the Virgin or God. However, the cult of worship of the Virgin is found in Fra Guittone d' Arezzo's sonnet of 1250, "To the Blessed Virgin Mary," and in Onesto di Boncima's sonnet of the same year, "Of the Last Judgment." Not until the end of the century is there a hint of the symbolic representation in the beloved; then it appears in "A Virgin Declares her Beauties" by Francesco da Barberino, who was born about the same time as Dante:

Lo! this is she who hath for company
The Son of God and Mother of the Son;
Lo! this is she who sits with many in heaven;
Lo! this is she with whom are few on earth.

Thus, among those poets whom Rossetti translated as being before the time of Dante, the concept of love that he found predominant arose primarily from a physical relationship; and the emphasis is on the suffering of the lover who seeks satisfaction. In such poems as d' Alcamo's "Dialogue" and Rinaldo d' Aquino's "A Lady in Spring," the woman willingly yields:

Now springtime makes me love,
And bids me satisfy
The lover whose fierce pain
I thought too lightly of.

Guido Guinicelli could often speak of love in terms of religious thought:

Brighter than morning star her visage glows;
She is beneath even as her Saint above;
She is as the air in summer which God wove. . . .

And, through such references, he suggests that he understands how man may discover God through the pure love of a woman: "No man could think base thoughts who looked on her"; but his verse never reveals the way to do so. His poetry, like that of many of his contemporaries, remains close to the troubadour tradition.

In the thirty-five poems by Guido Cavalcanti with which Rossetti begins the section on Dante's contemporaries, the same note of physical love is apparent; but a few of these verses indicate some relationship between earthly and heavenly love, such as "Of a Consecrated Image," and "To Guido Orlandi":

. . . God made her mortal on this ground.
And even herein His wisdom shall be found:
For only thus our intellect could know
That heavenly beauty which resembles her.

If the spiritual vision was to become the ultimate fulfillment of the physical, then death was the link; but Cavalcanti's reaction to death, much like Rossetti's late in his life, was one of remorse and fear that caused him to regret his "stubborn evil done." His canzone "A Dispute with Death" echoes in part the anguish sensed in many of the dark sonnets of Rossetti's *House of Life:*

> . . . look unto the end of youthful dreams.
> What present glory does thy hope possess,
> That shall not yield ashes and bitterness?

This attitude that death is the cessation of love and the loss of the beloved's presence appears, according to Rossetti's own statement, for the first time in Giacomino Pugliesi's "Of his Dead Lady." Unlike Dante, who found in Beatrice's death an elevation in her significance, Pugliesi found remorse; to Pugliesi, who is one of Dante's predecessors, love is physical; and death terminates the relationship. At the end of *Vita Nuova,* Dante is afforded a vision of the dead Beatrice, an experience which provides him with a "new perception born of grieving Love." Thus, the way is opened for Dante ultimately to find God and "Paradisal Love." These attitudes toward Death, as represented by Pugliesi and Dante, are found in the works that Rossetti translated. His own statement in his "The One Hope" indicates which view he came to accept—a view that he found in his translation of Boccaccio's "To Dante in Paradise." Boccaccio, like Rossetti, hoped that he might find his "one Hope's one name" after death:

> I know that where all joy doth most abound
> In the Third Heaven, my own Fiammetta . . .
> O pray her . . . that her prayers may never cease
> Until I reach her and am comforted.

Although the verse of Guido Guinicelli reveals much of the troubadour tradition, there is by 1220 in his "Of the Gentle Heart" a process of refinement that carries on the synthesis of romantic love and religious spirit that had begun earlier. Rossetti found in the verse of Cino da Pistoia a continued sense of the spiritual in the love concept. In the canzone to Dante "On the Death of Beatrice," Cino encourages his friend to find comfort:

> Look thou into the pleasure wherein dwells
> Thy lovely lady who is in Heaven crown'd,

Who is herself thy hope in Heaven, the while
To make thy memory hallowed she avails.

As with poets before him, Cino describes reunion after death in a physical sense. Again, writing of the death of Beatrice, he tells Dante not to grieve and thus offend

Against thy soul, which in the holy place,
In heaven, still hopes to see her and to be
Within her arms. Let this hope comfort thee.

Other poets in the group of Dante's contemporaries wrote of their beloved, attributing to them some religious significance, as does Dino Frescobaldi in his sonnet "Of the Star of his Love," in which he proclaims the birth of his lady from "heaven's pure height," a lady whose power causes all his sins to perish.

The vision of Love that Dante presented in his *Vita Nuova* and that the young Rossetti took so sincerely to his intense imagination was, therefore, not new with the Florentine. Dante had gathered together in a clear, orderly narrative form what had been evolving in the long years until his time as an implicit, unorganized concept. To this new synthesis Dante brought the powerful symbolic expression of a great poet, so that the young and inexperienced Rossetti was able to enter the experience with an intensity that is revealed in his forceful and poignant translation.

Actually, the sonnets and canzoni that Rossetti translated in the *Vita Nuova* contain many of the same themes and much the same treatment found in the verse of other writers of the time: the appearance of Love, signaling the beginning of the love experience; the sufferings of the impassioned lover; the request for kindness from the beloved; the lady's haughtiness; the death of the beloved and lamentations for her. Dante differed, however, in the narrative pattern he established. The easily recognizable poems that are clearly heirs of the troubadour tradition are woven together into a story by the framework of prose that clarifies his intense and heightened experience. The *Vita Nuova* also moves away from contemporary verse in its final vision of love; for Dante commemorates a love of the spiritual, a love that is ultimately released from the subjection of the sensual. Unlike other poets who anticipated a reawakening in Heaven of the love they had known on earth, Dante looks to a "new perception born of grieving Love"—a knowledge of the beloved's spirit that is "so subtile and so fine" that the earthly self fails to comprehend it. Finally, through the spirit of the beloved there is the last, sought-after comprehension of the spirit that is God. In the last sonnet of *Vita Nuova* Dante has a glimpse of this ultimate truth:

> Beyond the sphere which spreads to widest space
> Now soars the sigh that my heart sends above;
> A new perception born of grieving Love
> Guideth it upward the untrodden ways.
> When it hath reached unto the end, and stays,
> It sees a lady round whom splendours move
> In homage . . . when it tells me this
> Which it hath seen, I understand it not. . . .

Thus, Rossetti discovers in this work a vision of Love, whose statement in the poem may be traditional, but whose final interpretation in the prose tale raises that vision beyond anything sensed in Dante's contemporaries. Da Pistoia's hope for Dante was that, "in the holy place,/In Heaven," he may be "Within her arms"; but for Dante the hope transcends Beatrice herself. In his sonnet to Giovanni Quirino, "What He Feels at the Approach of Death," Dante states,

> . . . noting how in glorious quires agree
> The citizens of that fair citadel,
> To the Creator I His creature swell
> Their song, and all their love possesses me.
> So, when I contemplate the great reward
> To which our God has called the Christian seed,
> I long for nothing else but only this.

In these translations of Italian poets, the young Rossetti found all that was to constitute his later love dream. The poetic concept of love, mostly before Dante that had stressed the physical relationship even after death, fused in Rossetti's imagination with Dante's Beatrice-beatification. The result was, unfortunately, that Dante Gabriel never clarified his position; and, consequently, his poetry and art become a statement from an artist uncommitted to either view. This lack of sincere dedication, artistically and personally for Rossetti, was disastrous; for the view through his art and writings remains ill-defined; biographically, the results are apparent.

III *"The Blessed Damozel"*

In 1848, after leaving the Academy that spring, and before joining Brown in his studio in Marylebone, Gabriel, feeling discouraged about his hopes as a painter, sent to Leigh Hunt some of his verse in manuscript and asked for advice. The poems included "The Blessed Damozel," "Ave," and some of his translations. Hunt's reply about the original poems was that he "recognized an unquestionable poet . . . and beside your Dantesque heavens . . . admired the complete and genial round of your sympathies with humanity." Later, in a letter to his Aunt Charlotte, Rossetti, joking about Hunt's reference to "Dantesque heavens," said, "he refers to one or two of the poems the scene of which is laid in the celestial regions, and which are written in a kind of Gothic manner which I suppose he is pleased to think belongs to the school of Dante." [11] Written in 1847, "The Blessed Damozel," in its final result, as Rossetti says, is not Dantesque. It is not of the "Dantesque heavens," but rather of Rossetti's.

The theme of the poem is from the *Vita Nuova:* separated lovers are to be rejoined in Heaven. Dante had seen Beatrice in a vision after her death; ". . . there rose up in me on a certain day, about the ninth hour, a strong visible phantasy, wherein I seemed to behold the most gracious Beatrice, habited in that crimson raiment which she had worn when I had first beheld her. . . ." And the Damozel, like Beatrice, is envisioned by her lover. But the comparison between the two visions stops there; what Rossetti took from Dante fuses and changes under Rossetti's dream of young and ideal love. Unlike the disembodied spirit in the *Paradiso* that "turned back again to the eternal fountain," the Damozel

> . . . stooped
> Out of the circling charm;
> Until her bosom must have made
> The bar she leaned on warm. . . .

The conception of "The Blessed Damozel" came from Rossetti's reading Poe's "Raven," in which the sadness is that of the lover left alone on earth. Wishing to depict the other side of this theme, Rossetti pictures the sadness of the maiden in heaven. This approach, too, reverses the treatment by the early Italian poets who handle the death of the beloved from the lover's position.

This early poem is not religious, but it has a quiet, "spiritual" tone. The Damozel wears the white rose from Mary "for service meetly worn," and it is to the Virgin that the Damozel will take her lover when he joins her in heaven. They will "seek the groves/ Not once abashed or weak." And the Virgin shall approve and take the lovers before Christ, where the Damozel will ask that the two live "as once on earth/With Love." This inspired prayer of the Damozel, who wishes ultimately to find in heaven the love she had known on earth, is reminiscent of what Rossetti found in his translations of the Italian poets, and of what may be sensed in Keats' "Bright Star" sonnet, "Awake for ever in a sweet unrest,/ Still, still to hear her tender-taken breath,/And so live ever. . . ." However, the awareness of the sensual, the physical in the Keats poem, is absent in Rossetti's youthful statement of unchallenged idealism, of unexperienced love.

A large part of the delicate and quiet quality of Rossetti's poem is made possible by a vision that finds, as yet, its strength and identification in the untried relationship. As the sex relation is romanticized, so is the religious view. Of interest in this respect is Rossetti's sonnet "The One Hope" of 1870, the poem that ends the *House of Life* sequence, written in those years when the experience of actual enraptured love was foremost. In this sonnet the wish of the Damozel in "The Blessed Damozel" is repeated in the lover's wish that he may find after death "the one Hope's one name." What in 1847 is romanticized becomes a deeply felt experience in 1870; however, the vision appears to remain.

Furthermore, in "The Blessed Damozel" there are indications of Rossetti's future problem in conception. The delicacy of tone in the poem that has long caught the attention of readers is undeniable, but the success with atmosphere that Rossetti achieves becomes also a disguise for another fact: his lack of commitment to the vision. The highly wrought depiction in this poem at times is indeed graphic:

> Beneath, the tides of day and night
> With flame and darkness ridge

> The void, as low as where this earth
> Spins like a fretful midge.
> . . . .
> From the fixed place of Heaven she saw
> Time like a pulse shake fierce
> Through all the worlds.
> . . . .
> . . . the curled moon
> Was like a little feather
> Fluttering far down the gulf. . . .

The panorama suggests the ordered structure of Dante's world, identified in the hierarchy of the Chain of Being; and the personification of Time and the metaphors of gulf and tides seem to suggest an acceptance, in the poetic statement, of some systematized order of things. But these are devices, used much as in the hands of Poe, for atmosphere. As Rossetti never projected an ordered world-picture in his expression, so he also never consistently presented a philosophy, a cosmic view that expressed such an order.

What is implicit in his "The Blessed Damozel" is a concept of love that creates the impression of being idealized. There is a heaven; and souls of rejoined lovers mount up to God, passing like "thin flames"; and the Virgin sits among her handmaidens; but what we find is a highly romanticized portrait. The Virgin in Rossetti's poem might well be Keats' Angela in "The Eve of St. Agnes," bestowing her blessing on a Porphyro who comes, whether to Heaven seeking the Damozel, or to Madeline's chamber, except for one major difference; and this difference signals the stature of Keats over that of Rossetti—Keats sincerely believed in the fidelity and the ultimate transmuting and elevating power of Porphyro's love. Rossetti may have wished to believe, but finally did not.

The hesitation for Rossetti is between "two worlds," one not necessarily dead, but the other certainly "powerless to be born." Rossetti may, in his youthful imagination, poetically project the Damozel as Beatrice-like; but she is not Beatrice, and thus is not the visionary certainty. She becomes a sublimated metamorphosis of unfulfilled lover experience, described in the language of religion, which is the metaphor of the Dantesque vision. Yet in spite of any failure in conception, Rossetti's statement in this early poem is a masterpiece. But we should not confuse the success achieved in poetic statement and mood with the poet's structure of vision. "The Blessed Damozel" comes in the period of Rossetti's translations, and the poem is an amalgamation of what Dante Gabriel found in these early poems, the predominant sensual view of love and the spiritualized transvaluation in Dante. The symbols, metaphors, and ornaments of these love poems come down to Rossetti; but the young Victorian poet's vision of Woman is the Beatrice of Florence, who is pushed hopefully toward Paradise.

In "The Portrait," written at the same time as "The Blessed Damozel," the concern is with the pathos of the speaker-artist for his dead love. Like the "Damozel," this poem is in large part conceived on a plane of physical love of the earth; but the tone is colored by a sense of the supernatural. The feeling created through the language of the next to last stanza is like that of the religious passages found in Dante's *Vita Nuova* and is discovered again in later sonnets by Rossetti like "Love's Testament" (1869) and "Heart's Hope" (1871), as this quotation from "The Portrait" indicates:

> . . . How shall my soul stand rapt and awed,
> When, by the new birth borne abroad
> Throughout the music of the suns,
> It enters in her soul at once
> And knows the silence there for God!

Other lines from this poem such as

> . . . I shrined her face
> 'Mid mystic trees, where light falls in
> Hardly at all; a covert place . . .

are again like lines from "The Blessed Damozel":

> We two will stand beside that shrine . . .
> We two will lie i' the shadow of
> That living mystic tree
> Within whose secret growth the Dove
> Is sometimes felt to be. . . .

Certainly the atmosphere of "The One Hope" is here again recalled.

This sense of otherworldliness found in "The Portrait" again is a product of Dante Gabriel's early reading. The hint of the *doppelganger* theme in

> . . . many a shape whose name
> Not itself knoweth, and old dew,
> And your own footsteps meeting you,
> And all things going as they came

was a recurrent one with Rossetti; the belief must have made a poignant, lasting impression on his mind. It is manifest later in the "How They Met Themselves" sketch. But the important point is that Rossetti employs the devices of the supernatural to invoke the atmosphere that to him probably was confused with the aura of the religious or with what he conceived to be the mystical. The spiritual and the macabre blurred and somehow mingled in an imagination that straddled the Romantic and the Christian. Carried to an extreme, this merger of such strange conceptual partners can be seen in the ultimate distortion of the Beatrice figure in his 1877 "Astarte Syriaca." Mario Praz in *The Romantic Agony* makes the point that in Rossetti "there is to be found a conspicuous preference for the sad and the cruel . . . beside his Beata Beatrix stand magical, evil creatures," and Praz may not be far from the truth.[12]

The "religious" poems of this period, 1847–1849, include "Annunciation," "Ave," "Our Lady of the Rocks," "At the Sun-Rise," "Mary's Girlhood," "Vox Ecclesiae," and "On Refusal of Aid Between Nations." By 1848 Dante Gabriel was a skeptic, according to his brother, William. Both brothers shared their father, Gabriele's, religious attitude of holding no orthodox beliefs and of being indifferent to church dogma and ritual. Holman Hunt, in his *Pre-Raphaelite Brotherhood,* speaks of the young Gabriel: "In these days [of 1848] his inner life was untainted to an exemplary degree, and he worthily rejoiced in the poetic atmosphere of sacred and spiritual dreams that then dwelt within him in embryo, though undoubtedly some of his noisy demonstrations hindered many persons from recognising this inspiration at once." [13]

Hunt's reference to "poetic atmosphere" clarifies much about Rossetti, both at this early date and later. "The Blessed Damozel" and "The Portrait" poems mingle Dante Gabriel's early, youthful interest in the romantic, supernatural, and chivalric with whatever religious beliefs and feelings he may have accrued from the stern moral teachings of his mother, which included careful readings in the Bible. These two incongruous worlds found a point of common focus in his understanding of Dante in the *Vita Nuova,* a fusion that no doubt received encouragement under the influence of his father's researches and writings. Gabriel's sonnet of 1861, "Dantis Tenebrae," in memory of his father, highlights this strange, individualistic fusion. Speaking of receiving both his father's and Dante's name at his birth, he continues,

> . . . on thy son must Beatrice
> Decline her eyes according to her wont,
> Accepting me to be of those that haunt
> The vale of magical dark mysteries
> Where to the hills her poet's foot-track lies,
> And wisdom's living fountain to his chaunt
> Trembles in music?

R. D. Waller[14] responds to this strange mixture of ideas when he remarks that Rossetti "attributes to his reading of Dante an effect which was really more the product of quite other literature." The "vale of magical dark mysteries" becomes strangely, in Rossetti's imagination, a part of the concept of Beatrice. The measure of how far Dante Gabriel was to carry this idiosyncratic vision can be seen in his later sonnet and painting "Astarte Syriaca" (1877), in which the mysterious, pagan, sensuous Astarte of the Syrians offers "the infinite boon/Of bliss whereof the heaven and earth commune." She becomes the oracle "of Love's all-penetrative spell."

IV *Early "Religious" Poems and Tales*

Strangely enough, the majority of the religious poems of Rossetti's early years deal with a fairly orthodox view of the Virgin. His "Mary's Girlhood, I," written for his first picture, presents the human side of the Virgin, portraying her as a child and later as a young woman: "So held she through her girlhood; as it were/An angel-watered lily, that near God/Grows and is quiet." The second sonnet deals specifically with the symbols in that 1848 oil, and these verses appear on the frame of the painting.

Again, in "Ave" the same double view of the Virgin that occurs in "The Blessed Damozel" is found here: that of queendom: "'. . . the lady Mary is,/With her five handmaidens, whose names/Are five sweet symphonies. . . .'" But she is also a friendly intermediary: "'Herself shall bring us, hand in hand,/To Him round whom all souls/Kneel. . . .'"

The use of exact details, an esthetic principle acknowledged as part of the Pre-Raphaelite doctrine, gives "Ave" a striking graphic clarity found later in Rossetti's sonnets:

> That eve thou didst go forth to give
> Thy flowers some drink that they might live
> One faint night more amid the sands?
> Far off the trees were as pale wands
> Against the fervid sky. . . .

R. L. Mégroz,[15] commenting on this quality, says that "No other poet of the Victorian age . . . approached this magnificence in mystical religious poetry, where the splendour of image is one with subtlety of perception."

Reference to "mysticism" in Rossetti's work is, of course, difficult to support. Dante Gabriel's own use of the term later in life indicates its significance to him; for, when referring to the beryl stone in his "Rose Mary" ballad, he remarked, concerning the word "beryl," that it was the very word he wanted for the title of the poem: ". . . it is better than crystal in every way; it is more rhythmical, and has a greater seeming of mysticism in its sound." To Rossetti's brother, William, the "mysticism" in Dante Gabriel's work is not truly such: "He has been frequently termed a mystic, but he was almost the last man to be a mystic in the sense of disregarding or setting at nought the plain and obvious meaning of . . . [Dante], and transmuting it out of human passion, emotion and incident, into mere abstract speculation. . . . Into his idea of Beatrice he would condense as much spiritual as womanly motive force."[16]

In the verse and art of Rossetti's youth there is a spiritual quality, simple and often concrete in its presentation. The genesis of this tone arises, as William asserts, not out of a "transmuting" of the specific into the abstract, but out of a vision as yet unchallenged by threats to his dream and untainted by the distress of sensuality. The "mystery" of his youthful view was not that of his "Astarte Syriaca"; it is the bright, hopeful glimpse of idealized love that could provoke romantized verses and drawings of Mary-Beatrice.

The important question that Rossetti raises at the end of his "Ave"—"Soul, is it Faith, or Love, or Hope,/That lets me see her standing up/Where the light of the Throne is bright?"—again raises doubts concerning his mystic sense. The answer to this question is "Love," that, when it had grown into wisdom, would have with the eyes of Faith seen. But "Hope" however provokes the suspicion of fear; hope denies the mystical vision. Rossetti's "The One Hope" ends his *House of Life* on this same note of fear.

Dante Gabriel's own use of "mysticism" in his reference to the beryl stone in "Rose Mary" indicates that to him it was largely a matter of the supernatural, the mysterious and weird, the romantically ineffable. This highly imaginative bent of his appears in his two early prose tales, "St. Agnes of Intercession" and "Hand and Soul." Begun in 1848 while translating Dante's *Vita Nuova* and left incomplete, even after last efforts just before his death, the "St. Agnes of Intercession" reveals Rossetti's early germinal ideas and his uncanny capacity to prophesy his own future. This tale, as with "Hand and Soul," indicates the influence not only of Dante, but also of the *Stories After Nature* by Charles Wells, tales that Gabriel much admired. Furthermore, "St. Agnes of Intercession" reveals the impact of Poe, as Rossetti admits concerning "The Blessed Damozel." Like almost all the work of Rossetti, "St. Agnes" is "auto-psychological," a reference he made himself to this early prose piece as well as to Dante's *Vita Nuova*.

The tale begins with a reference to his own youth at home:

> Among my earliest recollections, none is stronger than that of my father standing before the fire when he came home in the London winter evenings, and singing to us in his sweet, generous tones . . . I used to sit on the hearth-rug, listening to him, and look between his knees into the fire till it burned my face, while the sights swarming up in it seemed changed and changed with the music: till the music and the fire and my heart burned together, and I would take paper and pencil, and try in some childish way to fix the shapes that rose within me.

Rossetti describes how the young painter of his "St. Agnes" tale met, fell in love with, and painted the portrait of his beloved, Mary Arden. Later, an art critic, seeing the portrait at an exhibition, remarks how like it is to the St. Agnes oil by Buccinuolo Angiolieri, a fifteenth-century Italian painter. The young painter recalls that he had once seen a reproduction of this painting, and he travels to Italy to find the original. When he finds the original, after much searching, he sees unquestionably the face of his own beloved; then, to his consternation, he finds, on locating a self-portrait by Angiolieri, his own face. He remarks, "That it *was* my portrait,—that the St. Agnes was the portrait of Mary,—and that both had been painted by myself four hundred years ago."

In this story, that William Rossetti refers to as "essentially . . . of metempsychosis," [17] the young painter learns that the lady who posed as St. Agnes for Angiolieri was beloved of that painter and had died while sitting for him for the picture. The details of this tale by Rossetti need not be traced to indicate the interesting fashion in which they later are fulfilled in Dante Gabriel's own life. This "metempsychosis" is repeated later in Rossetti's pen-and-ink sketch of 1860, "How They Met Themselves," drawn while he and Lizzie were on their honeymoon in Paris. In the same year the water color "Bonifazio's Mistress" was completed, depicting the scene of the death of the beloved as she sits for the St. Agnes portrait. In a letter to George Boyce, who acquired this water color, Rossetti indicated that the picture was intended to illustrate his own earlier "St. Agnes" tale.

Of particular interest in this selection, other than the *doppelganger* and metempsychosis ideas, is the reference by Rossetti, through his narrative figure, to his own early love vision. He has the young painter, who before verification suspects that the face of his own beloved is the one in the portrait by Angiolieri, remark: "How had I not at once recognized, in her I loved, the dream of my childhood? . . . The fact of the likeness was a mere casualty . . . but that which had cast the shadow of a man's love in the path of the child, and left the seed at his heart to work its growth blindly in darkness, was surely much more than chance." Later, in a dream delirium, in seeking his beloved, the young painter discovers instead the actual saint as she appeared in the painting; and he hears her say: " 'O Lord, it is more than he can bear. Spare him, O Lord, for her sake whom he consecrated to me.'" The young man, reflecting upon this vision, says, "I could sometimes almost persuade myself that my dream of that night also was not without a mystic reality." Thus in 1848, in this early youthful tale, Rossetti surrounds the vision of the beloved with a sense of the mysterious, the supernatural, the ominous, and the religious. The actual and the sainted ideal merge in a confused composite.

A clearer glimpse of Rossetti's ideal vision is afforded in his second prose selection, "Hand and Soul," written in late 1849 for the first number of *The Germ.* Arthur Benson[18] states that he believes "there exists no document more vital to the understanding of the principles on which Rossetti worked, and the lofty conception of art thus formulated." This assertion is perhaps true, as the statement involves Rossetti's conception of art, and that concept as it is inextricably concerned with his vision and woman's place in it. Again the tale concerns a young art student, this time Chiaro dell' Erma of Arezzo; and again the tale bears many close ties with Rossetti's own life.

At nineteen, Chiaro hears of the famous painter Giunta Pisano and decides to become his pupil. Once in the studio of Giunta in Pisa, Chiaro sees only forms "lifeless and incomplete"; and, suddenly in an exultant mood, he realizes, "I am the master of this man." Chiaro then determines to work out one of his thoughts and "let the world know him." But two factors make his ambitions incomplete, first, the realization "of how small a greatness might win fame," and, second, the attractions of pleasure and love. For a time, then, Chiaro's life is spent in the dissipations of youth until one evening, "being in a certain company of ladies, a gentleman that was there with him began to speak of the paintings of a youth named Bonaventura . . . adding that Giunta Pisano might now look for a rival." This news spurs Chiaro to reawakened ambitions, and for three years he works with great diligence until "his name was spoken throughout all Tuscany."

Even so, with fame, "the weight was still at his heart." In all the work he had completed "there had always been a feeling of worship and service. It was the peace-offering that he made to God and to his own soul for the eager selfishness of his aim." Again and again to Chiaro came a vision of the day when "his mystical lady (now hardly in her ninth year, but whose smile at meeting had already lighted on his soul,)—even she, his own gracious Italian

Art—should pass, through the sun that never sets, into the shadow of the tree of life, and be seen of God and found good." Chiaro realizes that the deepest desires of his spirit have been "no more than the worship of beauty," and he decides to paint nothing but works that have as their end "the presentment of some moral greatness."

His new aim produces only abstractions, and Chiaro "forgot the beauty and passion of the world." He no longer touched the hearts and spirits of his people. Finally an event occurs that prompts Chiaro to rediscover his true ideal and aim. On a feast day in Pisa, Chiaro watches the procession from the Church of San Petronio, and he observes a clash on the church porch between two feuding families of the city. In the altercation blood is cast on the walls of the church and runs down the frescoes of Peace painted there by Chiaro. Disillusioned, Chiaro murmurs to himself that "Fame failed me: faith failed me: and now this also, —the hope that I nourished in this my generation of men." While in his room, brooding, Chiaro suddenly experienced "a pulse in the light, and living freshness, like rain."

It is then that the figure of a woman appears, the symbol of his own soul. Clad in green and gray raiment, she seems to Chiaro "the first thoughts he had ever known . . . given him as at first from her eyes, and he knew her hair to be the golden veil through which he beheld his dreams."

William Sharp, in his study of Rossetti,[19] believes the speeches of the visionary woman to Chiaro "may be regarded as directly personal utterances applicable to [Rossetti] as an artist, and this I know from his own lips. . . ." The vision directs Chiaro to seek his own conscience, that of his heart, "and all shall approve and suffice." Casting her hair over Chiaro, she chastises him: "Thou hast said . . . that faith failed thee. This cannot be . . . who bade thee strike the point betwixt love and faith? . . . the heart must believe first." Her final directions to Chiaro are given: "In all that thou doest, work from thine own heart, simply. . . . Set thine hand and thy soul to serve man with God." Chiaro is told to paint the visionary woman as she appears to him: "Do this," she asserts, "so shall thy soul stand before thee always and perplex thee no more."

This painting by Chiaro, Rossetti pretends to have seen in Florence in 1847. The specific facts of the prose tale have led many to believe that Chiaro lived and that his oil is to be found in the Pitti gallery. But the confusion over the realism of details is of little import today; what draws readers to this story is the insight it provides into the early thinking of Rossetti. Written just before Elizabeth Siddal entered Dante Gabriel's life, "Hand and Soul" reveals early signs of the double-edged conflict that haunted Rossetti: a dedication to a vision, an ideal; and one also to the beauty and attraction of the flesh. The actual depiction of his soul's ideal may be found in the painting that Rossetti has Chiaro paint, just as we may say that Dante Gabriel's own vision is found in his oil "Beata Beatrix" of 1863, presenting a highly spiritualized conception of Miss Siddal, a portrait Rossetti inscribed with the date of Beatrice's death, June 9, 1290. As for Rossetti in this later portrait, as for Chiaro in his painting, the sense of a personal dream, tinged deeply with the aura of the religious, merges with the actual in the symbol of woman.

For the reader who knows Dante's *Vita Nuova,* many details in "Hand and Soul" can easily be traced. The reference to the ninth year of "his mystical lady" harks back clearly to Dante's use of the number nine. The description of the lady before Chiaro in green and gray raiment and with golden hair again recalls Beatrice. Rossetti completed this tale a short time after translating the Dante work. Chiaro's vision of this lady—Italian art, as she passes through the sun, into the shadow of the tree of life to be found good by God—is certainly an echo of Dante's concept of Beatrice; it recalls in verbal echoes and ideas Rossetti's own "The Blessed Damozel"; and it foreshadows much of the symbols and language of his later *House of Life*.

It is interesting to find so often in these early original works the depiction of young artists and of portraits of women, paintings which have attributed to them some supernatural and ominous significance. And it is also interesting to see Rossetti attempting to piece together a meaningful body of beliefs. In 1847, while yet at the academy school, disheartened with his own progress and disappointed in what his classes had to offer, in "Ave" he wrote: "Soul, is it Faith, or Love, or Hope,/That lets me see here . . . ?" As discussed earlier, the question remains as to the basis of Rossetti's belief. The answer should be "Love," as it eventually matures into "Faith."

In "Hand and Soul," written two years after "Ave," Rossetti

gives this very answer for himself through the message from the visionary woman to Chiaro: ". . . possess thy love in sufficiency: assuredly this is faith, for the heart must believe first." But in 1870 the indecisive third "Hope" appears in his sonnet, "The One Hope." And this same questioning note appears at the end, in 1881, in his poem "Insomnia," where "faith" is nullified by "hope":

> Is there a home where heavy earth
> Melts to bright air that breathes no pain,
> Where water leaves no thirst again
> And springing fire is Love's new birth?
> If faith long bound to one true goal
> May there at length its hope beget,
> My soul that hour shall draw your soul
> For ever nearer yet.

Here the lifelong vision is of the ultimate achievement of ideal love, where the actual becomes the final vision itself: Beatrice's salutation in Florence is repeated in "a finer tone" in her salutation in Paradise. However, where Dante saw the love of *Vita Nuova* transformed into the divine love of his *Commedia,* Rossetti managed only to mingle the two loves into a hazy romanticism that is ultimately unlike either.

This mingling, however, of Earthly Love and Paradisal Love in Rossetti's expression is a result of his visionary dilemma; unable to choose either one, since both made profound demands on him, and unable, like Dante, to journey as did Keats' "famish'd pilgrim" in "The Eve of St. Agnes," from the flesh to the spirit, Rossetti struggled distressingly in between. He hoped that death would somehow resolve what he could not, and "the wan soul in that golden air" would, peering breathlessly, find "the gift of grace unknown." His frustration in this dilemma can be interpreted also in the three-part oil, "The Salutation of Beatrice," that he completed late in 1859, shortly before his marriage to Lizzie.

V *Two Oils: "Dantis Amor" and "Found"*

Dante Gabriel painted the three oils on panels for a cabinet for the new "Red House" planned by the recently married William and Janey Morris. The two major pictures were of Dante and Beatrice: the first, their meeting and Beatrice's salutation in Florence; the second, their meeting and her salutation in Paradise.

Between these two oils was a third, a curious one called "Dantis Amor." In the center of this middle painting stands the figure of Love, dressed as a pilgrim and carrying various symbolical objects derived from the love mythology of Dante's *Vita Nuova:* the bow and arrow, and a clock face bearing the date "1290." This figure of Love is poised between the sun, depicted as the face of Christ, who looks down upon the face of Beatrice, as the moon. Diagonally across this painting runs the Italian inscription from the last line of Dante's *Commedia:* "By the love which turns the sun and the other stars."

In his translation of Dante's sonnet "On the 9th of June 1290," which he included in his *Early Italian Poets,* Rossetti may have found the idea for the figure of Love:

> Then, looking, I saw Love come silently,
> Habited in black raiment, smooth and new,
> Having a black hat set upon his hair;
> And certainly the tears he shed were true.
> So that I asked, "What ails thee, trifler?"
> Answering he said: "A grief to be gone through;
> For our own lady's dying, brother dear."

Doughty,[20] who speaks of the "Dantis Amor" in biographical terms, explains that Rossetti completed it at the time he struggled to accept the idea of his coming marriage to Lizzie. The "moon" for Doughty is the sickly, waning Lizzie, and the "sun" is Fanny Cornforth, toward whom Dante Gabriel was physically attracted. This interpretation is reasonable enough; but, beyond the facts of Rossetti's life, the "Dantis Amor" can also be interpreted as the inward struggle Rossetti experienced concerning his vision. The figure of "Love" stands between the two polar positions in Dante Gabriel's conception of Love: the spiritual, depicted in the "sun" and associated, as usual, with religious connotations; the physical, depicted in the mysteries of the "moon," and certainly understood in his 1877 poem "Astarte Syriaca":

> Mystery: lo! betwixt the sun and moon
> Astarte of the Syrians: Venus Queen
> Ere Aphrodite was. In silver sheen
> Her two fold girdle clasps the infinite boon
> Of bliss whereof the heaven and earth commune.

The intermingling in Rossetti's statement of the physical and the spiritual is apparent. The "infinite boon of bliss" is the sexual gift associated with the spiritual without actually becoming it; there is here, in the sense of "communion," Rossetti's usual vague, indefinite terminology that he employs when attempting to make manifest a sense of ultimate transcendence.

In those impressionable and formative years between the ages of seventeen and twenty-five, Rossetti worked, in summary, on the translations and on Dante's statement of youthful and idealistic love in *Vita Nuova.* His "The Blessed Damozel" came from this period, a poem whose vision shares much of the concept of Love held by Dante's own contemporaries. "The Blessed Damozel" may be a treatment in reverse of Poe's "Raven," but it also originates from the poetic statement of the fourteenth century that synthesizes the sensual, the emotion behind the cult of the Virgin Mary, and the idealization of the troubadours themselves; the final result, however, as Rossetti implied, is not Dantesque. Furthermore, in these early Italian poets Rossetti found another kindred feeling in their concern for visions and dream manifestations. As indicative in the early work of Rossetti, even before "The Blessed Damozel" and "Hand and Soul," there is a strong interest in the supernatural. The appearance of the visionary Beatrice to Dante after her death becomes as significant and real as Chiaro's vision of his own soul in "Hand and Soul," written about a year after Rossetti completed the translation of *Vita Nuova,* and just a few months before the appearance of Elizabeth Siddal.

Rossetti's profound empathic ability, which enabled him to share meaningfully the experience of Dante's young love, is also reflected further in other works of his early period before 1850. "My Sister's Sleep" of 1847 reveals his dramatic capacity for poignantly projecting into the sensitivities of others and thereby creating a sense of realism. In this poem again Rossetti's interest in religious topics mingles with the ever-present attraction to the mysterious and supernatural: on Christmas Eve the child's death is signaled by the sound of "a pushing back of chairs" in an upper room where the child lies.

But, as before in "The Blessed Damozel," Rossetti is vague in his poetic conception. Is the reader to employ the poetic meaning of the religious references to enlarge upon the central idea of the poem? As contributors to mood, such religious allusions are successful; but, when the critical eye falls upon the intellectual center of the poem, when that mood is separated from theme, the conception wavers. The suspicion is that Rossetti sought achievement of romantic mood, but that he cut across it poignantly by a contrasting intrusion of concrete details, as in

> Without, there was a cold moon up,
> Of winter radiance sheer and thin;
> The hollow halo it was in
> Was like an icy crystal cup.

The result is undeniably moving. But the important concern is the question of what significance Rossetti contributed to his religious facts beyond their function within this mood.[21] To answer this question is to untangle the confusion later on in poems where the mingling of the transcendental with the worldly is not so easily deciphered.

Rossetti's "Jenny," the story of a young man who gazes at and conjectures about a young prostitute as she sleeps the late hours away in her room, is again a poem that took the youthful writer outside his immediate experience. The early undramatic version of "Jenny" was later revised in 1859 by an older Rossetti, who believed the earlier attempt was beyond him in 1848, "A world I was then happy enough to be a stranger to." The theme of "Jenny" interested Rossetti as a subject for painting, and in the autumn of 1854 he began the oil "Found" that was to depict the prostitute discovered by her former lover as he passed early to market. The oil was worked on at various times throughout Rossetti's life, but at his death remained uncompleted.

Much of Rossetti's art at this time, the years 1848–1850, was encouraged by subjects from literature; but the literature that stimulated him most significantly was not his "town subjects," themes from everyday, realistic life, as he attempted unsuccessfully in "Found," but the writings of such men as Coleridge, Poe, Browning, Keats, and, mainly, Dante. The themes are those of the world of the supernatural, the romantic, and, briefly, the religious. Thus, what Rossetti chose to encompass in his poetry is found also in his art; together, the two modes of expressions reveal a similar imaginative world.

An early pen-and-ink sketch of 1848 from Coleridge's "Genevieve" depicts the lover as a lute player with his lady and reveals

Rossetti's interest in the chivalric, romantic world that, in his own conception, merges much of the atmosphere of his two influential worlds of the Arthur-medieval and the Dante-troubadour. In the same vein is his careful composition, in preparation for an oil never completed, of "Hist, said Kate the Queen" from Browning's "Pippa Passes," a scene again from the romantic world, this time of Kate as she sits among her maidens listening to a song by her enamored page. In this same year Rossetti completed other sketches from Poe's "Ulalume" and "The Raven," and two sketches using the Devil as a central figure, "Gretchen and Mephistopheles" and "Retro Me Sathana." His two important oils of religious themes are his "Girlhood of Mary Virgin" (1849) and his "Ecce Ancilla Domini" (1850), both reflecting his interest in the Virgin figure that formed a part of the composite symbol of the Ideal Beloved.

Of primary importance is Dante's *Vita Nuova,* which stimulated, in 1849, the first subject in his art drawn from Dante, his finished sketch "Dante Drawing the Angel," produced as a water color in 1853. A second sketch from Dante's work of this year is the important "The Salutation of Beatrice," which is repeated in oil in 1859. The middle drawing of Love, later in oil called "Dantis Amor" and there more complex in design, is in the 1849 sketch a simple drawing with Love bearing bow and arrows and carrying a down-turned torch. The scene of the meeting in Paradise became the subject of more than one separate drawing for Rossetti. These two early sketches from Dante are the first of a series of a dozen or more sketches and water colors to come in the next five years, the period of primary Dante influence on his art.

In the art and poetry of Rossetti through 1849 we can discover much about the inner life of the young man. At twenty-two—before the arrival in the spring of 1850 of Walter Deverell with the news of Elizabeth Siddal—Dante Gabriel was living and expressing a poetic ideal. His imagination peopled his world with figures who came garbed in the dress of the chivalric medieval world and who were strangely surrounded by an aura of the mysterious, the sacred, the visionary. As William later remarked, "juvenile amours, liaisons, or flirtations" were absent from Gabriel's youth.[22] The ideal vision of love was yet undisturbed by the anxieties of reality. The emotion of love, as yet repressed, was expressed in the chaste symbol of woman in Beatrice-Virgin.

CHAPTER 4

The House of Life: *Youth and Change*

BESIDES his translations, the work that critics believe is Rossetti's best is his *The House of Life* sonnet sequence. Graham Hough, in his excellent chapter on Rossetti in *The Last Romantics,* writes that "In many poets there is one complex of ideas that is central to their experience. They may write much on other themes, may even write better on other themes, but their deepest experiences are all concentrated more or less closely round one theme." [1]

Most certainly *The House of Life* is that "complex of ideas" so central to Rossetti's experience. In these one-hundred-and-three sonnets, poems that extend throughout Rossetti's lifetime, is revealed his "mythology" of love. Where a great deal seems derivative in Rossetti's early art and writings, these *House* sonnets become his own voice, yet colored by his early "masters" but now evocative of his inner self.

I *Style in the Sonnet Sequence*

In a letter to his mother of April 27, 1880, Gabriel enclosed a copy of his "The Sonnet," a poem which William Rossetti believed indicated Gabriel's "conception of the quality and function of the Sonnet as a form of poetic invention and composition" [2]: "A Sonnet is a moment's monument,—/Memorial from the Soul's eternity/To one dead deathless hour." Critical reaction has varied in response to this introductory poem to *The House of Life.* Paull Baum[3] believes the sonnet statement "leaves something to be desired," and William Sharp felt that, beyond the notable opening line, he could see in the poem "no special merit as a sonnet." [4]

It is true that this poem confronts the reader with some of the complexities and obscurities of Rossetti's later style; for, like the later oils, his language had a way of developing "long necks" and "pronounced lips." However, "The Sonnet" does attest to one thing: Gabriel's conscientious devotion to the sonnet form. Into *The House of Life* he poured all his energies and care. The sequence reveals the "conception" that he spoke of to Hall Caine, that "Fundamental brainwork, that . . . makes the difference in all art." [5] Rossetti once noted that Algernon Swinburne composed rapidly, but with him "the case was different." Poetry demanded a great deal of him: "I lie on the couch, the racked and tortured medium, never permitted an instant's surcease of agony until the thing on hand is finished." [6] When he wrote his sonnets, he gave to the poetic creation a degree of intensity and extended attention not always expended in his art work.

The charge of obscurity against the sonnet group has been a long-standing one. In Sharp's early study[7] of the sequence, 1882, this observation is made: ". . . not infrequently is the reader arrested by obscurity of expression, by a too subjective *motif*. . . ." Furthermore, Sharp insists, the sequence concerns itself with a narrow range of the emotions of life; the group may better be called "a House, not of Life, but of Love." Joseph Knight, in his study of Rossetti,[8] 1887—generally a most appreciative evaluation—hints kindly at the difficulty in the collection: "That passages are obscure, and that the sequence of idea is not always to be traced is true." Both Sharp and Knight, however, did little to examine the broader poetic ideas in these sonnets; but their concern for the difficulties of the reader was ultimately acknowledged by William Rossetti in 1889: "I have more than once been told that the verses by my brother . . . of *The House of Life*, are very difficult of interpretation." [9]

In his discussion of Gabriel's paintings and writings in *Designer and Writer*, he appended a prose paraphrase of the *House* sonnets. Later, in 1906, in his own *Reminiscences* William again recalls his 1889 paraphrase: "I added to the volume a literal prose-version or amplification of the sonnet-sequence . . . for the benefit of those . . . who opined that the sonnets themselves are not easy to be understood . . . I find most of the sonnets are plain enough, and that others . . . are accessible to a sympathetic mind." [10]

Arthur Benson[11] in 1904 acknowledges problems, particularly in Rossetti's later sonnets, which "are not clearly and freshly seen, but veil themselves dimly under heavy ornate fabrics, beneath which the outline tends to disappear." The second important paraphrase of the *House* sonnets was written in 1928 by Paull Baum, who, following the direction of William Rossetti in 1889, writes that "Rossetti often disguised his meaning under a cloud of gorgeous phrasing. Yet the meaning is there, if one choose to disengage it." [12]

The obscurity that these critics have acknowledged arose most probably from two sources within Rossetti: one was a matter of his craftsmanship; the other, a "philosophical" problem arising from Rossetti's ultimately unresolved perplexity in his "mythology" of love. To Rossetti, the sonnets were a primary means of expressing concerns most close to his heart; and he reworked them again and again. William records in his diary of May, 1869: "Gabriel has written several new sonnets. His practice with poetry is first to write the thing in the rough, and then to turn over dictionaries of rhymes and synonyms so as to bring the poem into the most perfect form." [13]

Joseph Knight comments that the young Rossetti was "employed at the British Museum reading romances of chivalry, in the hope to 'pitch upon stunning words for poetry.' " [14] This concern for the individual word in his work is indicative of Rossetti's "perfecting" care that he gave his poetry. Still later, William wrote about Gabriel's labors: "In the execution he was always heedful and reflective from the first, and he spared no after-pains in clarifying and perfecting. He abhorred anything straggling, slipshod, profuse, or uncondensed. He often recurred to his old poems, and was reluctant to leave them merely as they were." [15]

Aside from these biographical statements, the poems themselves attest to Dante Gabriel's labor. So much care was given the sonnets that Rossetti's constant revisions have erased hopes for an accurate study of growth in his poetic style and expression. Because some manuscripts are available, but are scattered, many in private hands, making a worthwhile study is an almost impossible task. Evidently Rossetti was dissatisfied with his poetry, as with his paintings; for he constantly altered earlier work. His art patrons often learned too late what this constant urge to revise meant, after they had responded to Rossetti's pleas to return paintings for touching up. Sometimes the changes in poems were for the better; at other times, his later inclinations toward ornate and tortured expression dulled the brilliance of earlier work. Sonnets bearing early dates show signs of later mannerisms, and some late poems have flashes of the earlier simplicity. About the most we can offer, when discussing Rossetti's periods of poetical growth, are general statements about the common characteristics of each stage. One fact is, however, indisputable: as Rossetti grew older, his expression became more elaborate.

A few general remarks can be made about the nature of Rossetti's early and late style as revealed in the *House* sonnets. The occurrence of run-on lines, hyphenated words, forced accents on rhymes, varied metrics, personifications and interjections, "balance" in the line, and effective language is evident in the work of all periods of his career. But the fact remains that his early style is often more direct, has more monosyllables, employs less simile and metaphor, and is expressed in a more prose-like language involving less use of imagery than his later manner. The later style has more variations in the rhyme scheme, particularly in the 1869–1871 period; more polysyllabic and compound words; more inversions in syntax; a more complex punctuation; and more alliteration. Actually, then, the main difference between early and late style is one of language and syntax. In the later poems, sound and form frequently cast the idea in shadow. The result has been a constant occurrence of the charges of obscurity in the critical history of *The House of Life.*

The trouble can be easily spotted and easily illustrated by those who wish to make a case for this charge. As early as September, 1882, just a few months after Rossetti's death, Principal Shairp in an article on Dante Gabriel's poetry complained that the sonnets were "buried beneath a load of artificial diction and labored metaphor." [16] Arthur Benson says much the same: "gorgeous word-textures, strange tapestries of language." [17] Such lines as "the cloud-foaming firmamental blue," "as instantaneous penetrating sense," "whereof the articulate throbs accompany," and "seizure of malign vicissitude" demonstrate what Paull Baum has said are the considerable lapses in the *House* poems because of Dante Gabriel's probable attempt for compactness which produced a troublesome crowding in the already tight sonnet form.[18]

II *"Bridal Birth"*

But to cite such language complications is not to suggest that Rossetti lacked control over the sonnet structure, for few would quarrel with the evaluation that Dante Gabriel is one of the finest

English sonneteers. Rossetti's desire for unity and compactness in the fourteen lines did at times evolve into lines of heavyhanded language; however, there are many sonnets which illustrate a masterful ability, for example, Sonnet II, "Bridal Birth":

> As when desire, long darkling, dawns, and first
> The mother looks upon the newborn child,
> Even so my Lady stood at gaze and smiled
> When her soul knew at length the Love it nurs'd.
> Born with her life, creature of poignant thirst
> And exquisite hunger, at her heart Love lay
> Quickening in darkness, till a voice that day
> Cried on him, and the bonds of birth were burst.
> Now, shadowed by his wings, our faces yearn
> Together, as his full-grown feet now range
> The grove, and his warm hands our couch prepare:
> Till to his song our bodiless souls in turn
> Be born his children, when Death's nuptial change
> Leaves us for light the halo of his hair.

This poem, dated 1869 by William Rossetti, falls in the period of Rossetti's life and creativity which Doughty[19] calls "regenerate Rapture" when the love for Janey Morris clearly emerges. Doughty sees in the sonnet a description of the genesis of love between Dante Gabriel and Mrs. Morris. Furthermore, this poem becomes another of many in the sequence that "breathes a heavy atmosphere of defensive secrecy, as in some clandestine passion constantly menaced by a hostile world." It is likely true that this sonnet, read in the autobiographical sense, indicates this particular attitude in Dante Gabriel's love; but the poem reveals additional significance upon scrutiny. "Bridal Birth" is typical of the fifty-two poems in Part I of *The House of Life* that were written in this 1869–1871 period of poetic renaissance in Rossetti's life.

Various characteristics of the troubadour poetry that Rossetti found so prevalent in his Italian translations are here: Love is personified in his typical godlike role; the woman is associated with the Virgin; and the presence of the physical is colored by religious terminology. Also, this sonnet is representative of the chief images found in Rossetti's love poems. There are actually two sets of births portrayed in "Bridal Birth." First is the birth of Love, and then the birth of lovers as children of Love. Furthermore, there is here as in most of Rossetti's love statements another two births, that of the heart and the higher love of the soul.

The light-darkness imagery is employed to illustrate both sets of births and to give the sonnet an undeniable unity. Implicit in the sonnet is a well-worked-out metaphor of marriage and birth. Love springs from the "marriage" of the Lady and "lover," and they in turn are reborn spiritually from the union of Love and Death. In the octave "mother" and "my Lady" are paralleled, as are womb and "soul," "newborn child" and "Love." In the sestet Love prepares the couch for the parents of Love, and they become, as "bodiless souls," the children of Love. As such, they gain an illuminated spirituality from the power of "light" of Love's force or "halo of his hair." What Rossetti's images depict is the concept of ultimate spiritual love. The love in the octave that bursts "the bonds of birth" is physical; the love of the sestet is made spiritual through "Death's nuptial change."

The light imagery is consistently handled throughout. First, it is desire that "long darkling, dawns"; and the darkness gives way to light. Love, as a child, "quickening in darkness," is born after "a voice that day/Cried on him." In the sestet the imagery again occurs, thus giving the sonnet unity. Physical love now shadows the parents with his wings, and again desire comes, except that it is cast in less physical terms. Rossetti's frequent use of music imagery occurs here: Love's song calls forth the greater love of united souls and the lovers enter the intense light of love's highest gift. Through this imagery of light and music Rossetti hints at a mystical experience, if such experience can be described generally in Rossetti's work as a transcendence of physical into spiritual. At least the language and suggested framework of such an experience are present; but whether or not Rossetti finally was able to accept in faith the experience is another question.

Such use of imagery to depict the mystical is certainly not new with Rossetti's work. George Ford[20] studies the influence of Keats on Rossetti's work, but what he does not touch on in his examination of verbal echoes in Rossetti from *Endymion* is the imagery from that poem that Rossetti studied so closely, a poem he called "a magic toy, fit for the childhood of a divine poet." In *Endymion*, Book I, lines 777–807, Keats describes the mystical experience as the "fellowship divine,/A fellowship with essence." He begins with the imagery of music, the "Eolian magic from their lucid wombs," and moves "Into a sort of oneness" where, at the height of the achievement, "hangs by unseen film, an orbed drop/Of light, and that is love." The same imagery is repeated in the love experience and ultimate transcendence in "The Eve of Saint Agnes."

La Vita Nuova affords another source for "Bridal Birth." In Dante's "Love and the Gentle Heart" sonnet we find a close parallel to Rossetti's sonnet:

> Love and the gentle heart are one same thing,
> Even as the wise man in his ditty saith:
> Each, of itself, would be such life in death
> As rational soul bereft of reasoning.
> 'Tis Nature makes them when she loves: a king
> Love is, whose palace where he sojourneth
> Is called the Heart; there draws he quiet breath
> At first, with brief or longer slumbering.
> Then beauty seen in virtuous womankind
> Will make the eyes desire, and through the heart
> Send the desiring of the eyes again;
> Where often it abides so long enshrin'd
> That Love at length out of his sleep will start.
> And women feel the same for worthy men.

As in "Bridal Birth," the heart is the place from which Love arouses from sleep. It is "Nature" for Dante that "makes" Love and the "gentle heart," and Love resides in the heart until beauty is seen; and "desire," a while "enshrin'd," will call Love from slumber.

Dante's reference in line two to "the wise man in his ditty" is to Guido Guinicelli and his poem "Within the Gentle Heart Love Shelters Him," a poem Rossetti also translated and included in his *Dante and His Circle*. The imagery in Rossetti's poem is even more apparent in the Guinicelli poem, in a few representative lines:

> Within the gentle heart Love shelters him
> As birds within the green shade of the grove.
> Before the gentle heart, in nature's scheme,
> Love was not, nor the gentle heart ere Love,
> For with the sun, at once,

So sprang the light immediately; nor was
Its birth before the sun's.

The essential difference between Rossetti's conception and that of Dante in *Vita Nuova* and of Guinicelli is that neither of the Italian poets suggests the transcendence through physical love to the spiritual. What Dante ultimately finds at the end of *Vita Nuova* is "a new perception born of grieving Love" that reveals "a lady round whom splendours move," and not a promise of "The One Hope" fulfilled where the Blessed Damozel receives her earthly lover and they "live as once on earth/With Love." Aside from this difference of "mythology," which measures the vast ideational chasm between Dante and Rossetti, the poems share a common vocabulary.

Other poets represented in *Dante and His Circle* wrote in much the same vein. Cino da Pistoia, in his sonnet concerning Dante's dream in *Vita Nuova,* writes,

With thy heart therefore, flaming outwardly,
In humble guise he fed thy lady so,
Who long had lain in slumber . . .
. . . .
. . . heart should unto heart true service bring.
But understanding the great love-sickness
Which in thy lady's bosom was conceived,
He pitied her. . . .

The canzone "Of His Change Through Love" by Pannuccio dal Bagno employs the light-darkness imagery to illustrate the presence of love or its absence:

Lady, since I conceived
Thy pleasurable aspect in my heart,
My life has been apart
In shining brightness and the place of truth;
Which till that time. . . .
Groped among shadows in a darken'd place. . . .

"Bridal Birth" is the most typical in imagery and in emotion of the love poems of Part I, written mostly between 1869–1871. This sonnet, like many others, is alive with sensuous terms; but Joseph

Knight's charge of fleshliness is not supportable. The latent force of vibrant sensuality is there, just below the surface of the poem's statement; but the success of this sonnet, as of many others by Rossetti, lies in his ability to keep the strength of such language in the service of his poetical idea. As such, this relationship of language and idea becomes a part of the "metaphysical" aspect of some of Rossetti's poetry, where his imagery is able to yoke together the idea and the feeling, so that the statement passes into the more perceptible realm of the emotions without sacrificing the distinction of its own outline.

Like Dante, Rossetti frequently uses religious overtones in his love sonnets, as can be found in line 8; the implication there in "Quickening in darkness, till a voice that day/Cried on him, and the bonds of birth were burst," is one of God's bringing forth light from chaos and of the virgin birth of Mary, where "him" attributes to Love, the child, an almost divine significance, who, in a "nuptial change" through Death, elevates the "yearning faces" to "bodiless souls" and leaves "for light the halo of his hair."

Dante had in his *Vita Nuova* attributed to Beatrice a religious significance. In his sonnet "I Felt a Spirit of Love Begin to Stir," Dante pictures the arrival of Beatrice, preceded by the Lady Joan, who "was called by many *Primavera*" and who is compared to John the Baptist, "who went before the True Light." There are other religious connotations attributed by Rossetti to the lady of *The House of Life*. In Sonnet III, "Love's Testament," a poem full of religious terminology, Rossetti sees the beloved work the lover's deliverance, yielding him grace; and, like Christ's harrowing of hell, the beloved draws up his "prisoned spirit" to her own soul. "Love's Testament" is reminiscent of Rossetti's portrait of the Blessed Damozel, whose love in heaven for her lover was conceived by Dante Gabriel as a continuation of an earthly love, a love that heaven will approve. Clearly Rossetti is not depicting Christian doctrine in this early poem, but how far he asks his reader to go in accepting the "validity" of his religious conception is not clear, mostly because Rossetti is not clear himself. This is true of "Love's Testament"; the inconsistency between the aura invoked by the Christian symbolism he employs and the purely Romantic framework in which these symbols appear has long disturbed and confused many readers.

Where Dante clearly distinguishes between the "myth" of

fleshly love and the validity of his theology, Rossetti confuses the two; and readers of the *House* poems wonder what significance to attribute to his imagery. Thus, the more important reason appears for the obscurity attributed to the *House* sonnets: the unresolved perplexity in Dante Gabriel's own mind concerning his *mystique* of love.

One thing is certain about Rossetti: to him love was a necessity. When he speaks of love, his is not the voice often found in the poems of some of his Italian predecessors, who were wont to display their verbal nimbleness and ingenuity. Rossetti's voice was sincere, serious. The essence of life was for him the presence of love, and its absence was death. In an early sonnet of 1848, "The Choice, I," he writes,

> Now kiss, and think that there are really those,
> My own high-bosomed beauty, who increase
> Vain gold, vain lore, and yet might choose our way!
> Through many years they toil; then on a day
> They die not,—for their life was death,—but cease;
> And round their narrow lips the mould falls close.

The expression in this poem shows signs of the awkwardness of the young poet, but the idea remains basic and paramount throughout the sonnets he was to write. This poem "The Choice, I" appears now in Part II of the *House* sequence, probably for a good reason. Most of the sonnets of Part I of the 1869–1871 period share a unity of impassioned statement and power and of attitude that this earlier poem does not have. And the imagery of the Part I love poems is consistent, a stylistic trait of later maturity and rapture that the 1848 poem lacks.

III *"Love's Last Gift"*

The last sonnet of Part I, LIX, "Love's Last Gift," is interesting for a couple of reasons: first, its assertion about "genuine" love; second, its reassertion of idea from "Bridal Birth." Regardless of whether or not Rossetti was successful in earnestly accepting the concept of spiritual transcendence beyond physical love or in getting his imagery to illustrate this transcendence with conviction, he did believe without question in the importance of love in life.

In Sonnet LIX, dated 1871, Love speaks to the lover, saying that love, whether open and acknowledged by others or hidden and clandestine, is good if it be genuine. Rossetti may have Browning's "Statue and the Bust" in mind, as well as circumstances in his own life. In any event, regardless of the genesis of this poem, the assertion in it is consistent with the love statements of the *House* sequence:

> Love to his singer held a glistening leaf,
> And said: "The Rose-tree and the apple-tree
> Have fruits to vaunt or flowers to lure the bee;
> And golden shafts are in the feathered sheaf
> Of the great harvest-marshal, the year's chief,
> Victorious Summer; aye, and 'neath warm sea
> Strange secret grasses lurk inviolably
> Between the filtering channels of sunk reef.
>
> All are my blooms. . . .

The imagery of summer, fruition, light, warmth, and water occurs; and these images depict, as in other *House* poems, the passionate condition of love. Some of Rossetti's finest, most striking lines employ the summer and sunlight images. In line 6, summer is "Victorious." In Sonnet LXXXII, he implores the lovers to "sup with summer"; the day of Sonnet XXX has been "Summer's paramour/ Sun-coloured to the imperishable core."

Furthermore, this last sonnet in Part I of the sequence is interesting in its restatement of ideas from "Bridal Birth." Part I commences with a rather philosophic statement in "Love Enthroned," in which Rossetti finds Love superior to other primary life factors, such as Truth, Hope, Fame, and Youth. Reminiscent again of Keats in his Grecian urn ode, Rossetti believes "Love's throne was not with these; but far above/All passionate wind of welcome and farewell/He sat in breathless bowers they dream not of. . . ."

Sonnet I, unlike the majority in Part I, does not involve a dramatic instance through which the idea is presented; instead, in "Love Enthroned" the idea is directly stated. The second sonnet, "Bridal Birth," does present a "dramatic" situation in which the lovers participate, and thus it surpasses the first in intensity. Sonnet LIX, like the first in Part I, is again a "philosophic" statement, thus giving to this first section of *The House of Life* a frame. Like Sonnet II, this last poem discusses the transcendence of love. It is the lord of Love who explains,

> ". . . all sweet blooms of love
> To thee I gave while Spring and Summer sang;
> But Autumn stops to listen, with some pang
> From those worse things the wind is moaning of.
> Only this laurel dreads no winter days:
> Take my last gift; thy heart hath sung my praise."

In offering the laurel, its last gift to the faithful, Love gives immortality. The salvation sought in Sonnet III, "Love's Testament," is here found. Part I begins with the "birth" of Love, who in turn bestows the "change" through the nuptial with Death. Part I ends with the gift given. He who has sung the music of love finds at last "for light the halo." Unfortunately, however, "those worse things the wind is moaning of" dominate mood and idea in Part II, and the promise of Part I is lost; and the lover is left at last to beg for "The One Hope." Love's laurel that "dreads no winter" may be beyond life, but whether it is to be found there is ultimately dubious.

The House of Life is the poetic chart that indicates this rise and fall in Rossetti's mystic hopes. The sequence affirms that Rossetti sought his vision, not in his art as he wrote in his own youth in "Hand and Soul," but in women. And the hint of a failure in his vision comes early in the sequence. Sonnet IV, "Lovesight," provides evidence for Caroline Spurgeon's belief [21] that Rossetti did not attain the spiritual vision because he became entangled in sensuous beauty:

> O love, my love! if I no more should see
> Thyself, nor on the earth the shadow of thee,
> Nor image of thine eyes in any spring,—
> How then should sound upon Life's darkening slope
> The ground-whirl of the perished leaves of Hope,
> The wind of Death's imperishable wing?

Love's laurel here becomes the "perished leaves of Hope," the prayer of hope that ends the *House* sequence. The validity of vision becomes enmeshed in the net of the physical. It is true that the octave of this poem does state that the soul is discoverable through the immediacy of the flesh, ". . . when . . ./Close-kissed and eloquent of still replies /. . . my soul only sees thy soul its own." However, the sestet confirms that once the physical agent is gone, the "hope" goes as well.

Rossetti also states as much rather clearly in Sonnet V, "Heart's Hope": "Lady, I fain would tell how evermore/Thy soul I know not from thy body, nor/Thee from myself, neither our love from God." The two worlds of flesh and spirit are not to be identified apart. This poem of 1871 continues the romantic myopia of "The Blessed Damozel" of twenty-four years before. Heaven, it is true, is a place where "souls mounting up to God/Went by . . . like thin flames," but those souls ultimately become young, warm-bosomed maidens seeking their lovers.

There have been a few critics who have insisted that Rossetti was a mystic, that what he sought was the knowledge of the mystery that lay beyond desire. F. W. H. Myers in "Rossetti and the Religion of Beauty" [22] is perhaps the earliest writer to insist upon this interpretation; C. M. Bowra reechoes Myers' position in his *The Romantic Imagination* (1949).[23] Myers' article came at an appropriate time, 1885; a great deal of the criticism after Rossetti's death was yet derogatory, emphasizing the fleshliness of his poetry. The charge from Robert Buchanan's review of Rossetti's *Poems* in the October, 1871, *Contemporary Review* still left its mark on the public's mind. Myers finds in Dante's *Vita Nuova* "the very gospel and charter of mystical passion," and what Myers postulates is that Rossetti makes a successful transfer of that "gospel" to his own expression. To support this thesis, Myers illustrates from Rossetti's *House* sequence. It is interesting that the poems used are almost totally from the 1869–1871 period and are passionate love statements which heavily employ religious terminology.

However, Myers does admit that the "transfiguration" in Rossetti's view ". . . is effected not so much by any elevation of ethical feeling, as by the mere might and potency of an ardent spirit which projects itself with passionate intensity among things unreachable and unknown." In his discussion Myers does not touch on much in Part II of the *House* poems except "The One Hope," which closes the collection, and "Soul's Beauty," which was written for the oil "Sibylla Palmifera" and as a companion piece to "Body's Beauty," written for the oil "Lady Lilith."

Bowra, who does discuss some of the darker pieces from Part II, relates them to the "gospel" of Beauty in Rossetti's *House* as signs of a "fear that [Love] could not last. . . ." The hint of this fear, as indicated, appears early in Sonnet IV, and itself confirms what Bowra finds; but to confirm such a fear is also to confirm that Rossetti's faith lay essentially with the flesh itself, and not with the eternal which was found only when the flesh lost its import.

IV *The Charge of Fleshliness*

Critics have not been united about this evaluation of the role of the flesh in Rossetti's poetic statement. Graham Hough writes, "Perpetually tormented by the irreconcilability of the unsensual love he had idealised and the love of the senses, he tries to identify them . . . he simply turns his own confused and all too human conception of love into the highest value, and calls it God . . . no real reconciliation between them is ever achieved." [24] However, R. L. Mégroz, in his excellent 1929 study, insists that Rossetti ". . . deliberately confuses physical life with psychic life because the most urgent experience he knew of love was that soul and body were not strictly to be separated. Why should he distinguish between them, if love of a woman's body set his heart on fire?" [25]

Rossetti himself was keenly aware of the presence of the sensuous in his poems. In April, 1870, when the publication of his *Poems* was imminent, Dante Gabriel wrote to Professor C. E. Norton, who then was in Florence and had invited Rossetti to visit him there:

> I hope you will soon get my volume of poems. . . . Some friendly hands are already at work on reviews of it: Morris for *The Academy*—Swinburne for the *Fortnightly*—Stillman for an American paper—and others . . . I hope that when you get my book you will agree with me as to the justness of my including all it contains. I say this because there are a few things—and notably a poem called *Jenny*—which will raise objections in some quarters. I only know that they have been written neither recklessly nor aggressively . . . but from a true im-

pulse to deal with subjects which seem to me capable of being brought rightly within Art's province.[26]

Rossetti's lifelong fear of public censure is revealed in his concern for poetic treatment that may offend; but he went on to say in this letter to Norton that he awaited "the final result without apprehension"; however, circumstances clearly indicate otherwise. This same reticent attitude was earlier reflected in his hesitancy in sending his Aunt Charlotte a copy of *The Early Italian Poets.*

Rossetti's sense of foreboding was right; Buchanan in his attack on the *Poems* fell upon "Jenny," as he does other poems: "We detect its fleshliness at a glance; we perceive that the scene was fascinating less through its human tenderness than because it, like all the others, possessed an inherent quality of animalism." [27]

Rossetti had been careful in the preparation of his poems for the 1870 volume, for most of them had been reworked and had appeared in privately printed *Trial Books.* Moreover, opinions of friends and fellow artists had been carefully sought out. Sonnet VIa, "Nuptial Sleep," which was earlier called "Placata Venere," was one poem that particularly concerned Rossetti:

> At length their long kiss severed, with sweet smart:
> And as the last slow sudden drops are shed
> From sparkling eaves when all the storm has fled,
> So singly flagged the pulses of each heart.
> Their bosoms sundered, with the opening start
> Of married flowers to either side outspread
> From the knit stem; yet still their mouths, burnt red,
> Fawned on each other where they lay apart.
>
> Sleep sank them lower than the tide of dreams,
> And their dreams watched them sink, and slid away.
> Slowly their souls swam up again, through gleams
> Of watered light and dull drowned waifs of day;
> Till from some wonder of new woods and streams
> He woke, and wondered more: for there she lay.

This poem, which appeared in 1870, was omitted from the completed *House* sequence in 1881; but William Rossetti returned it to the collection in his 1904 edition. When Dante Gabriel wrote his brother about "Nuptial Sleep" in 1869, when proofs were being read for a privately printed test volume, William's first reply was to include the sonnet "by all means—at any rate, so long as the collection remains private." In a later letter William wrote, concerning the original title, "Placata Venere," ". . . I think you might *perhaps* reconsider the title, which appears to me a nearer approach to indecorum than anything in the sonnet itself." [28]

In another letter to William, Dante Gabriel was concerned about the phrasing in the last line of the octave. Earlier it had read: "chirped at each other." "Chirped" was changed to "moaned" and later to "fawned." Buchanan, in his unjust critical method of detaching single lines from context and of centering on particular poems as being representative of the whole, singled out "Nuptial Sleep" for sharp censure; and he charged Rossetti with "putting on record . . . the most secret mysteries of sexual connections" solely to reproduce "mere animal sensations." Buchanan concluded his remarks on the sonnet with the epithet "trash."

"Nuptial Sleep" is one of three closely related sonnets written in 1869–1870 in the 1881 edition: it continues the idea of Sonnet VI, "The Kiss"; and its content is continued in Sonnet VII, "Supreme Surrender." In the octave of "Nuptial Sleep," the imagery is much like that found in "Bridal Birth." In the intense consummation of physical love, the lovers sink away "lower than the tide of dreams," conceivably to a sense of physical death; and from this "death" their "souls swam up again" to light and to "new woods and streams." And the lover awakens, as is hoped for in the final *House* sonnet "The One Hope," to find "the gift of grace." In this sonnet, as in "The One Hope," the imagery of flowers, water and light is employed to represent the transcendence. And what is presented through imagery and "dramatic" episode in the octave of "Nuptial Sleep" is stated directly in the octave of "The Kiss":

> I was a child beneath her touch,—a man
> When breast to breast we clung, even I and she,—
> A spirit when her spirit looked through me,—
> A god when all our life-breath met to fan
> Our life-blood, till love's emulous ardours ran,
> Fire within fire, desire in deity.

The same evolution of child, man, and child-spirit found in "Bridal Birth" is present. Sonnet VII, "Supreme Surrender," other than in the line "and the deep/Calls to the deep," does not suggest the spiritual implications found in the preceding two poems. "Supreme Surrender" seems to be simply a poem stating the pleasure of physical attainment; but, following through from Sonnet VI, to VIa, and then to VII, the reader may trace a suggested cycle in the love adventure: the transcendence of physical to spiritual is begun in Sonnet VI, is attained in VIa, and is lost again in a return to physical reality and subsidence in Sonnet VII.

The devastating impact on Rossetti of Buchanan's infamous attack on *Poems* and Dante Gabriel's controlled and successful reply in "The Stealthy School of Criticism" in the *Athenaeum* of 1871 have been amply considered in various biographical studies. Responding to Buchanan's charge of nastiness against "Nuptial Sleep," Rossetti insisted the poem was but a single part of the total *House* group and was not representative of the entire collection.

He then referred his readers to other poems such as "Love-Sweetness" where he insists that physical love was made meaningful only in its relation to the spirit: "the swift beat/And soft subsidence of the spirit's wing." Dante Gabriel continued, concerning "Nuptial Sleep," ". . . one charge it would be impossible to maintain against the writer of the series in which it occurs, and that is, the wish on his part to assert that the body is greater than the soul. For here all the passionate and just delights of the body are declared . . . to be as nought if not ennobled by the concurrence of the soul at all times."

Twentieth-century literature has moved a considerable distance beyond the daring of poetic statement of the Victorian era found in such artists as Swinburne and Rossetti. As a result, critical concern at present centers primarily on the artist's conception, not on his subject matter. Does Rossetti's poetry support his own assertion that the "delights of the body" are "ennobled by the concurrence of the soul"?

In the awkwardly expressed sonnet of 1848, "The Choice, I" Rossetti maintained that life without love was a death; but to find love in life was to discover death. In Sonnet XLVIII, "Death-in-Love," he asserts that Love and death are one; earthly love becomes subservient to mortality. Ample evidence exists in the *House* sonnets, however, both in imagery and specific statement, that through this earth-bound love heaven was to be discovered. And occasionally glimpses of that ultimate paradise were grasped in this life. In his 1881 group of three sonnets, "True Woman," Rossetti maintains, in the third poem of that group, "Her Heaven," that the promise of everlasting youth in heaven can be partly realized on earth by lovers who have accepted the end of earthly love, like the loss of all other facets of life, in death.

The decline in Rossetti's health in 1866–1867—his concern over weakening eyesight and his growing problem with insomnia and hydrocele—brought on long periods of deepening melancholy. In September, 1868, he visited at Penkill Castle in Ayrshire with Miss Alice Boyd and Bell Scott, and in increasing despondency, drinking more heavily in hopes of finding sleep, Rossetti often talked of suicide. His friends tried encouraging Dante Gabriel to write poetry again. In November, William reported that his brother was revising some old poems and writing new ones. The series of four sonnets "Willowwood" came at this time, which commenced his period of poetic revival. Doughty[29] regards these sonnets as a celebration of the ending of the years of severance and frustration in Rossetti's love for Mrs. Morris. Behind these biographical matters lies Rossetti's poetic statement about love. The imagery of "Willowwood" is again that of "Bridal Birth." Accompanied by the music of love, the image of the beloved rises out of the dark waters; and, at last, as in "Nuptial Sleep," it slips away again like "drowned waifs of day"; and from the darkness the images are seen within the aureole of Love. The celebration in these sonnets may also be for love born again, out of the darkness of physical death, into the "moan of pity and grace" of Love's spiritual light.

Often the circumstances of life frustrate the fulfillment of love and negate any possibility of the birth of the higher spiritual experience. This idea becomes a primary concern in Part II of the *House* group, but it is also found in Part I in such a poem as Sonnet LIV, "Love's Fatality." Such negation is reechoed in LV, "Stillborn Love," whose octave is antipodal to "Bridal Birth":

> The hour which might have been yet might not be,
> Which man's and woman's heart conceived and bore
> Yet whereof life was barren . . .
> . . . .
> Bondchild of all consummate joys set free . . .
> It somewhere sighs and serves, and mute before
> The house of Love. . . .

"Life's iron heart" of "Love's Fatality" has prevented the birth of love in this life so that the birth must await eternity when ". . . wedded souls now hand in hand/Together tread at last the immortal strand/With eyes where burning memory lights love home." Almost all the last poems of Part I suggest this idea and prepare for the primary voice of melancholy in Part II and for the prayer for the discovery of "The One Hope" at the end of the sequence itself.

Thus, a second strong note of Part I, other than that of those love poems which depict the transcendence of physical consummation into spiritual achievement, is one of suspicion and fear about what death would offer. The sacred trinity of *The House of Life* is Life, Love, and Death. Sometimes in his doubt Rossetti encourages the lovers to seize what happiness they may. In Sonnet XLIII, "Love and Hope," he advises,

> Cling heart to heart, nor of this hour demand
> Whether in very truth, when we are dead,
> Our hearts shall wake to know Love's golden head
> Sole sunshine of the imperishable land;
> Or but discern, through night's unfeatured scope,
> Scorn-fired at length the illusive eyes of Hope.

Again, in his use of light imagery, the only light of eternity is that of the golden head of Love, the halo of "Bridal Birth" and the aureole of "Willowwood."

In Sonnet XLIV, "Cloud and Wind," the poet asks "And if I die the first, shall death be then/A lampless watchtower whence I see you weep?" Here the Romantic optimism of "The Blessed Damozel" is blighted; the earlier "gold bar of Heaven," from which the beloved leans out, now becomes the "lampless watchtower" from which the lover may fail to see the death of the beloved when she ". . . too learn [s] that all is vain/And that Hope sows what Love shall never reap." The suspicion that Love only pretends to offer hope is again hinted at in "Sleepless Dreams" where Rossetti questions concerning night: ". . . would Love feign in thee/Some shadowy palpitating grove that bears/Rest for man's eyes and music for his ears?" He concludes that night is indeed "A thicket hung with masks of mockery."

In "Last Fire" the phases in the cycle of love are cast in the imagery of the seasons. Although the achievement of love is seen as "Summer's paramour,/Sun-coloured to the imperishable core" Rossetti asserts that "Many the days that Winter keeps in store,/Sunless throughout, or whose brief sun-glimpses/Scarce shed the heaped snow through the naked trees."

Rossetti's hope rather fully dominates the early poems of Part I. The sunlight of earthly love continues into the night of death where one finds his love made eternal.

> . . . as the traveller triumphs with the sun,
> Glorying in heat's mid-height, yet startide brings
> Wonder new-born, and still fresh transport springs
> From limpid lambent hours of day begun;—
> Even so, through eyes and voice, your soul doth move
> My soul with changeful light of infinite love.

Soon, though, this assurance of "Soul-Light" and the "deathless dower" of the "close-companioned inarticulate hour" of love become suspect.

The poems of questioning increase so that Part I ends within the circle of engulfing darkness, relieved only by the almost determined assertion of hope in "Love's Last Gift." The fact that the summer of love promises no continued joy in the coming winter becomes the major note of Part II, as seen in "Hoarded Joy": ". . . let us sup with summer, ere the gleam/Of autumn set the year's pent sorrow free,/And the woods wail like echoes from the sea." This sonnet is dated 1870, written in the period of Rossetti's "regenerate rapture." At the very moment of impassioned statement of eternal love, there is also the ominous sound of despair. That idealized love of the Blessed Damozel for her lover which is to be continued with God's blessing in heaven becomes at last a matter of *carpe diem.*

By 1854 the first period of Rossetti's poetic career was completed. He had written by that time such works as "The Blessed Damozel," "Dante at Verona," "The Bride's Prelude," "Jenny," "Sister Helen," "My Sister's Sleep," "Stratton Water," his translations in *Dante and His Circle,* "Hand and Soul," and "St. Agnes of Intercession." The completion of his first period of painting is signaled by his oil "Beata Beatrix" in 1863. His second period of poetic creation comes in 1869 and runs through 1871, ending with Buchanan's pamphlet on the "Fleshly School" in May, 1872. In this period many of the *House* sonnets were composed, plus "Troy Town," "The Cloud Confines," "The Stream's Secret," "Eden Bower," "Rose Mary," and "The Orchard Pit." Concerning these poems of the second period, Mégroz[30] remarks that one characteristic is "an awareness of mystery," which, this critic maintains, ranges from a mystical sense to that of Romanticism; and this trait ties both the earlier and the later periods of poetry together. Most certainly the Romantic aspect is stronger than the mystical in Rossetti's poetry up to 1871.

V *Rossetti's Art, 1850–1863*

A look at the pictures by Rossetti from the early works of about 1850, much influenced by Dante, through 1872 reveals again much the same course of expression as found in the *House* poems, which followed the earlier youthful poems and prose of Rossetti's first period. In 1850 the oil "Ecce Ancilla Domini" appeared with several water colors in the next few years, these using Dantesque subjects: "Beatrice Denying Her Salutation," 1851; "Giotto Painting Dante's Portrait," and "Dante and Beatrice in Paradise," 1852; "Dante Drawing the Angel," 1853; "Paolo and Francesca" and "Dante's Vision of Rachel and Leah," 1855; and "Dante's Dream" (early version), 1856. The period of the Dante art subjects ends with the "Beata Beatrix" oil in 1863.

This group of works under the direct stimulus of the Dante influence ranges, therefore, from about 1850 to 1856 and was partly set in motion following Rossetti's discouragement with religious subjects when his "Ecce Ancilla Domini" brought him unfavorable critical response. Rossetti turned in the 1850 period then to literature for his stimulation. His early enthusiasm for Browning encouraged sketches from "Sordello" and "The Laboratory."

The Morte d'Arthur subjects begin in 1854 with the watercolor "Arthur's Tomb," when Rossetti had become acquainted with Malory. In what Marillier[31] calls a "strange, sad little water-colour" is depicted Lancelot bidding a last farewell to Guinevere; he is seeking a kiss from the queen as he leans across the tomb of Arthur. In this imaginary scene is found a sign of Rossetti's early interest in the haunted, clandestine, unhallowed love. As indicated earlier, this interest is reflected in the "Found" oil and "How They Met Themselves" (1851).

We may conjecture—and are encouraged by biographical events in Rossetti's own life and by interpretation found in his poetry and art to do so—that Rossetti's delay of over ten years in marrying Lizzie may in part have been a result of his growing disillusionment with her when she was unable to fulfill his dream of the Beatrice-Virgin ideal projected into her. It is interesting to note in his pictures of this 1854 period a shift often from the idealism of the Dante subjects to the interest in frustrated or illicit love in the Morte d'Arthur period. In early 1854 Rossetti is concerned with "Found" and with "Paolo and Francesca." In August, he wrote to William Allingham that he was at work on a design on Hamlet and Ophelia, "deeply symbolical and farsighted, of course." The same sense of one haunted appears in the exquisite design for a woodcut, "The Maids of Elfen-Mere," done by Rossetti in 1855 for William Allingham's *Day and Night Songs.*

In 1856 Rossetti designed five illustrations for the famous Moxon edition of Tennyson, each an exquisite work reflecting Rossetti's interest in medieval subjects. Each drawing, lavish in detail and evidently creating some confusion for Tennyson himself, depicts the close-quartered, secret sense found in other works of this period. Again the Arthurian subjects are found in "Sir Galahad at the Secret Shrine" and in the sketch of the dying Arthur attended by the weeping queens.

The year 1857 was the one of the Oxford frescoes and of many Morte d'Arthur and medieval subjects: "Damsel of the Sanc Grael," "Chapel Before the Lists," "Blue Closet," and "Wedding of St. George." In many of these works there seems some reawakening of the earlier idealism depicted in the Dantesque art, one encouraged perhaps by meeting and falling in love with Janey Burden at Oxford. The sense of close secrecy that Doughty senses in many of the late *House* sonnets is perhaps reflected earlier, before Rossetti's later period of poetic activity, in these drawings, many of which are scenes of intense crowding. The pen-and-ink study for Queen Guinevere, part of the Oxford fresco work, is done from Jane Burden in 1857; and this work hints at some of the later characteristics of Rossetti's art in the handling here of such features as the lips, eyes, and neck of Miss Burden. As Miss Siddal figured often in the earlier Dante art period, so does Janey Morris emerge in the Arthurian period and in the work of the years when Rossetti was writing his love poems for the *House* sequence.

Marillier records that the last and most important work for 1859 was Rossetti's "highly-finished little head in oils, called 'Bocca Baciata.'" [32] This painting is important for a number of reasons: the small portrait is the first significant endeavor in oil for Rossetti since the 1850 "Ecce Ancilla Domini." The reception of that earlier work probably discouraged Dante Gabriel from working in oils, and the reaction was compounded doubtlessly by the ever-persistent problem for him of his real lack of preparation after his rejection of the academy school classes. But from 1859 Rossetti began an earnest attempt to establish a reputation as an artist in oils. Ruskin, in his interested support of Rossetti's career, long had argued that oils brought more money than water colors. By 1859 some new assurance in the handling of technical skills had come for Rossetti. Arthur Benson[33] records that only commissions for water colors, that brought the always needed "tin" for mounting debts, induced Dante Gabriel to adopt that medium. By 1865, in a response to a published statement that he had abandoned oil painting, Rossetti insisted he considered himself primarily concerned with oils.

The completion of "Bocca Baciata" in 1859 signaled not only a significant shift to oils, but also a shift in content. Rossetti began to turn increasingly to sensuous portraits of women. Holman Hunt insists that Rossetti's Llandaff triptych of 1860 was begun "at the turning point from his first severity of style to a more sensuous manner." [34] The "women and flowers," as Bell Scott was to refer to Rossetti's work of this period, become the major expression in his painting from 1860 on. The Blessed Damozel and Beatrice gave way to Lady Lilith and Monna Vanna.

Oswald Doughty records a passage from the diaries of Scawen Blunt, in which John Henry Middleton, a friend of Rossetti, remarked that Dante Gabriel ". . . was addicted to loves of the most material kind both before and after his marriage, with women, generally models, without other soul than their beauty. It was remorse at the contrast between his ideals and his real loves that preyed on him and destroyed his mind." [35]

In his art, the "Beata Beatrix" of 1863 is representative of the early period of idealism. In his poetry, many of the *House* sonnets of 1869–1871 attempt a similar mystical view of love. However, in the case of both painting and writing, the expressions in both mediums that were to come in the years ahead reflect Rossetti's growing loss of his poetic vision.

CHAPTER 5

The House of Life: *Change and Fate*

THE mood of despair and fear that shares a voice with the love ecstasy of Part I of *The House of Life* becomes primary in Part II, entitled "Change and Fate." Doughty finds even in a poem like "Bridal Birth," which purports to describe the genesis of love, the menace of a hostile world. This pervasive gloom seems generated both by a dread of loss of love and by a haunting awareness of having failed in life.

I *The Personal Voice of the Sonnets*

William Rossetti writes in *Designer and Writer* (1889)[1] that the sonnets in *The House of Life* were mostly "occasional": "some incident happened, or some emotion was dominant, and the author wrote a sonnet regarding it." However, Dante Gabriel endeavored to deny the personal nature of his poetic statement in these sonnets, but recent studies, such as Doughty's *A Victorian Romantic,* adequately support William Rossetti's statement. Rossetti himself in his introductory poem to the series, "The Sonnet," acknowledges the personal voice in the sonnet form. Furthermore, the first two sonnets of Part II, "Transfigured Life" and "The Song-Throe," make it quite clear that the poet's personal feelings become the basis of expression:

> . . . in the Song, the singer's Joy and Pain,
> Its very parents, evermore expand
> To bid the passion's fullgrown birth remain,
> By Art's transfiguring essence subtly spann'd.

So readers of the *House* may well assume it is Rossetti's voice they hear.

Rossetti, who read and respected the work of Coleridge, wrote that "the sense of the *momentous* is strongest in Coleridge; not the weird and ominous only but the value of monumental moments." This observation was made well before Dante Gabriel wrote "The Sonnet" in 1880; and it is interesting to find verbal echoes in the poem's "moment's monument." Furthermore, Rossetti's respect for the "momentous" in Coleridge is for him a discovery of literary and emotional kinship with the poet. J. B. Beer, in *Coleridge the Visionary,* discusses two roles in which the Romantic artist often found himself; one of these is that of "fallen angel," where he has a sense of a "fall," making maturity a period of disillusion.

Coleridge shared this role, Beer indicates, but the essential difference between Coleridge and Rossetti is one of scope. The "fall" for most Romantic writers like Coleridge was macrocosmic; for Rossetti, it was microcosm-centered. Disillusionment for Dante Gabriel may often be poetically conceived in language and in imagery of religious connotation, suggesting a cosmological evaluation; but the momentous experiences remain Rossetti's own. God, as a philosophic reference extending out from and containing the individual awareness, did not concern Rossetti, other than to vaguely suggest an achievement of some sort beyond love. Nor were the problems of the political or economic world immediately about him. The Crimean War, Tractarianism, and evolution found no place in the concerns expressed in Rossetti's sonnets.

The distress in the loss of an earlier innocence for Blake or of a "visionary gleam" for Wordsworth becomes in part for Rossetti the growing suspicions about the validity of his youthful love ideal. R. D. Waller,[2] in his somewhat poetic explanation, sees Rossetti's fate as not unlike that of the Lady of Shalott: "He lived in a world of shadows and reflections, and happily wove them into his web, until maturity took him down to Camelot and broke the web for ever." Dante Gabriel's dilemma, for Waller, is largely a result of the warring elements in his personality—his own highly emotional nature against the more ascetic training and awareness from his mother and from his reading in Dante. Doughty,[3] who makes much the same point, designates the emotional ambivalence reflected in Rossetti's life and work: the pronounced pleasures in the physical and the rapturous exaltation of the mystical are reactions finding a strange, dubious harmony in the sacramental vision of the love ideal.

The seeds of Dante Gabriel's later disillusionment find encouragement in this inner conflict; and, as discussed earlier, "Hand

and Soul" (1849) foreshadows the later problem. Like his own creation, Chiaro, who dedicates himself to the vision of his own soul that stands before him in the guise of a Beatrice, Rossetti attempted to be true to his own dream. In all probability, Elizabeth Siddal came to the young, inexperienced Rossetti in 1850 as a fulfillment of the vision itself. But the sickly woman, often argumentative, and growing more demanding on Rossetti as the years passed, paled before him. There were other loves as well, more fleshly ones; and the immediacy of physical gratification collided with the etherealized image of woman as a symbol of what rose above the flesh. The gesture of sacrifice to that image—his placing his verses with the dead Lizzie—was also later violated. The haunting memory of the lost Lizzie, both as woman and symbol, remained with Dante Gabriel. His beautiful portrait of her in "Beata Beatrix" (1863) is testimony enough of how significantly he had conceived the love ideal to lie in her.

In Sonnet LXI, the second of two poems which introduce Part II and which concern Rossetti's view of poetic creation, we learn that Apollo "for thy soul/Fledges his shaft"; and in Sonnet LXII, "The Soul's Sphere," we discover just what is "the soul's sphere of infinite images": "Tragical shadow's realm of sound and sight/Conjectured in the lamentable night." In the sestet of this poem, Rossetti wonders whether these images of the soul forecast

> The rose-winged hours that flutter in the van
> Of Love's unquestioning unrevealed span,—
> Visions of golden futures: or that last
> Wild pageant of the accumulated past
>   That clangs and flashes for a drowning man.

Thus Part II of *The House of Life* begins, and the question raised is both primary and unresolved. In his 1869 "Willowwood" poems Rossetti sees the beloved sink back into the dark waters; and, as in his "Nuptial Sleep" of the same year, the promise of this drowning and sinking is that of "Bridal Birth," where Love yields his final grace in "Death's nuptial change." In "The Soul's Sphere" of 1873 the answer is not certain any longer. Do the images of the soul promise the perfect love or the "clangs and flashes" in a final dying? The same question had been asked in 1871 in "Love and Hope" in which Rossetti wonders whether, when dead, he shall awake "to know Love's golden head . . ./Or but discern, through night's unfeatured scope" the delusion.

The indecisiveness that Rossetti may have felt in attempting to discover his ideal fulfilled in Elizabeth Siddal can be found in "The Landmark," written fifteen years before "Willowwood," which uses imagery that appears in the later sonnet. Doughty[4] reads Rossetti's recognition in this poem as part of his wavering attitude about Lizzie; for Rossetti remarks that he has failed to drink from the well, but instead scatters his own reflection with pebbles. The sonnet "Birth-Bond," also of 1854, hints at Rossetti's idealism, his concept of a love not yet discovered:

> . . . when first I saw you, seemed it, love,
> That among souls allied to mine was yet
> One nearer kindred than life hinted of.
> O born with me somewhere that men forget,
> . . . .
> Known for my soul's birth-partner. . . .

However, his sonnets "Lost on Both Sides" (1854) and "A Dark Day" (1855) clearly indicate that his suspicions were established, and they reveal his own awareness of failing to discover his ideal in the world of actuality, the "prayer found vain."

The contrasting pair of sonnets "Soul's Beauty" and "Body's Beauty" were written originally in 1869 for the oils "Sibylla Palmifera" and "Lady Lilith" and appeared in *Poems*, 1870, among "Sonnets for Pictures." Later they were transferred to *The House of Life* when Rossetti saw in them the appropriate contrast he understood so well himself between the flesh and the spirit. Though in "The Birth-Bond" (1854) Rossetti still hoped for a coalescence of flesh and spirit, in his sonnet "Farewell to the Glen" and in his long poem "The Stream's Secret" (1869), he no longer earnestly expected such a union. Both poems were begun under the impetus of his visit to Penkill Castle, Ayrshire, in the fall when Dante Gabriel, almost blind and highly distraught, lay writing near the Penwhapple in the Penkill glen. In his "Farewell to the Glen," Rossetti writes: ". . . do thou rather say 'farewell' to me,/Who now fare forth in bitterer fantasy/Than erst was mine. . . ."

His "The Stream's Secret" is even more revealing of his despondency. In the poem he calls upon the water of the stream to speak to him of his love, and the mood and idea are reminiscent of "Willowwood":

> Say, hath not Love leaned low
> This hour beside thy far well-head,
> And there through jealous hollowed fingers said
> The thing that most I long to know.

As fancy brings forth the image of the beloved in "Willowwood," in "The Stream's Secret" memory recalls "our hearts deep-shrined in love." In his love he found his glimpse of the ideal:

> And from the living spirit of love that stands
> Between her lips to soothe and yearn,
> Each separate breath shall clasp me round in turn
> And loose my spirit's bands.
> . . . .
> . . . on the unmeasured height of Love's control
> The lustral fires are lit.

But the exigencies and disappointments of time intervene and all is in vain:

> All the sad sum of wayworn days;—
> Heart's anguish in the impenetrable maze;
> . . . .
> Alas! shall hope be nurs'd
> On life's all-succouring breast in vain.

At last, realizing that the water shall yield no secret to him, he concludes that death may be the way to love: "On deathlier airs the hour must come/Which to thy heart, my love, shall call me home." In death, Rossetti understands, Love will gather "the water in his hand"; and they that drink shall alone know love.

Recent criticism of this poem sees in it Rossetti's involvement in his love for Janey Morris and not a plea to join Lizzie in death, as earlier studies suggested. The poem also becomes the poet's assertion that death may be the sole way to find love's fulfillment. He asks of himself the question concerning suicide in "Death's Songsters" (1870): "Say, soul, are songs of Death no heaven to thee?" Rossetti's melancholy grew in this period, accelerated by chloral, sleeplessness, Buchanan's attack, and his fear of blindness; and in June, 1872, he attempted suicide.

The years 1869–1872 were indeed a period as much of despair and contemplation of death as of the expression of passionate love. In Sonnets XCIX and C, "Newborn Death," 1869, Rossetti wonders, "How long, O Death?"; and he asks when he shall "reach the strand/Of the pale wave" and drink from the hollow of Death's hand. Dante Gabriel once believed that Life, like a faithful wife, had borne him the children of Love, Song, and Art: "Love, the child once ours; and Song, whose hair/Blew like a flame and blossomed like a wreath;/And Art, whose eyes were worlds by God found fair."

Has Life destroyed these, only to yield him now the child of Death?—and the answer is yes. One alternative to this harshness of life Rossetti offers in "Hoarded Joy" (1870), but it is by no means a solution to or an acceptance of his problem: seize what little happiness may appear before the winter of despair and loss comes.

Few of the poems in Part II actually touch directly on love; but these few are, in tone, much in keeping with the majority of sonnets. By far the larger number of poems present Rossetti's general evaluation of life and the way in which he has lived it. As "Newborn Death" indicates, Life offered him Love and his work as poet and artist—and then destroyed the gifts. For the loss of love there is but "hope." In his last sonnet, "The One Hope," which closes the *House* sequence, he ponders: when all man's desires and endeavors go finally to death and "all is vain," "What shall assuage the unforgotten pain/And teach the unforgetful to forget?"

To this question Rossetti offers no answer. There is no forgetting the vision itself, although it is lost or even proved doubtful. To discover that "I and this Love are one, and I am Death" does not seemingly diminish hope, nor does the suspicion "that all is vain/And that Hope sows what Love shall never reap." Rossetti's last word on his love vision is a desperate plea:

> . . . when the wan soul in that golden air
> . . . .
> Peers breathless for the gift of grace unknown,—
> Ah! let none other alien spell soe'er
> But only the one Hope's one name be there.

Thus *The House of Life* does not end with an affirmation but with a fearful prayer. The joyful conviction of his youthful damozel was gone. Life bears the gift of Love and reclaims it, and the poet can only hope that his ideal is true and that the gift is again restored everlastingly. There is a note of appropriateness about Waller's metaphor: in maturity Rossetti was taken to Camelot and his web broken.

II *Sonnets of Personal Failure*

In that maturity, though, Rossetti offers no final "one hope" for the retraction by Life of the other gifts of Song and Art. As early as 1853, in "Known in Vain," Rossetti was well aware of his own personal failures. His dedication in "Hand and Soul" of 1849 was paling, but Hunt and Millais by 1853 were finding advancement, and their futures promised recognition and success. Letters of this period by Dante Gabriel to his family indicate his restlessness, indecision, and lack of specific direction. There are requests for money from William and from the good Aunt Charlotte. In the autumn he writes his mother that he is busy "but somehow it seems impossible to finish anything."

In January he had written "Known in Vain" which William had described as a poem "of a man who in youth has been feeble in will, indolent and scattered, but who, when too late, wakes up to the duty and the privileges of work." William regarded this sonnet as autobiographical, and admitted Dante Gabriel's desultory nature. Their father, William states, was irritated and "found occasion to reprehend Dante sharply, and even severely; and to reprehension my brother was at all times more than sufficiently stubborn." [5] The Rossetti family in these years were in a "very straitened money-condition"; and William relates that Dante Gabriel, in his indecisiveness about the future, even considered a job as railway telegrapher. "Luckily for all parties concerned," William writes, including the railway passengers, his brother's inquiry came to nothing.

It is interesting in this early poem of self-reproach that Rossetti, in the extended simile that makes up the statement of "Known in Vain," should see the failure of work and will as similar to failure in love: two lovers, recognizing too late their feelings, come at last to sit "Together, within hopeless sight of hope." In 1853, Lizzie's health was failing, there were increasing financial problems, and

Rossetti's hopes for his art were not materializing. Doughty[6] believes that perhaps the intense construction and the crowding in Rossetti's drawings of this period, such as "Arthur's Tomb," "The Wedding of St. George," and "Dante Drawing an Angel," reflect the withdrawal of Dante Gabriel and Lizzie from the growing anxieties of the outside world to the seclusion of Chatham Place. There is in this work a sense "of love's futility in the presence of a malign fate."

In November, 1850, after having met Miss Siddal in the spring, Rossetti was to write in "Autumn Idleness," one of few poems that treat directly the details of the natural scene: ". . . I still lead my shadow o'er the grass,/Nor know, for longing, that which I should do." His failure to grasp opportunities and to set resolutely to work continued, and his sense of aimlessness is voiced in "Known in Vain." In the summer of 1853 he went to Newcastle to visit Bell Scott, having secured another loan from Aunt Charlotte. In part Dante Gabriel was already fleeing the necessity of deciding about the marriage for which Lizzie was beginning to press. It was on this trip that he wrote "The Hill Summit," Sonnet LXX, which describes a reaching and a passing of a significant boundary. The octave is expressed rather fully in religious terminology:

> This feast-day of the sun, his altar there
> In the broad west has blazed for vesper-song;
> And I have loitered in the vale too long
> And gaze now a belated worshipper.

Here again his imagery supports the idea; light is representative of the love ideal, a light that now begins to subside. The holiness of that ideal is clearly couched in the vocabulary of worship. In the sestet the darkness is promised: "And now that I have climbed and won this height,/I must tread downward through the sloping shade/And travel the bewildered tracks till night."

Rossetti definitely intended symbolic implications in this sonnet. In a letter of September 15, 1869, to William, in which he offered some alterations in the poem, he remarked that "the symbolism being thus more distinct," he considered transferring the sonnet to his *House* group. Doughty[7] reads in the poem "a record of bitterness of spirit" and considers the work another indication of Rossetti's thoughts about suicide. The assertion of having "loitered . . . too long" is one of many recognitions in Part II of personal failure. The religious terms and imagery, so reminiscent of the love poems of Part I, suggest that the failure may well be that of his inner vision.

His deepening sense of remorse for his lack of achievement never abated. By 1862 in "Lost Days" the despair is profound indeed. William, in paraphrasing this sonnet, explains the central idea: "To lose one's days, to squander one's time, is like committing suicide in instalments. Every lost day is a . . . murdered self." His neglect and unfulfilled hopes will haunt him through eternity, Rossetti believes. "A Superscription," 1868, continues this vein of expression: "Look in my face; my name is Might-have-been: / I am also called No-more, Too-late, Farewell."

This anguish takes on the scope of a curse in "He and I" and reverberates with Rossetti's long interest in the theme of one haunted by himself. His early *doppelganger* sketch of "How They Met Themselves" is reechoed in this sonnet of 1870. What Rossetti discovers in it is a new "self" that has come to occupy his existence. In place of his former, happy self, there now stalks a dejected being who with a moan becomes "the sighing wind's auxiliary." Where in the past Dante Gabriel "drew living light from one continued year," he now finds in the "soul's atmosphere" only death. Out of his confused emotions, engendered doubtlessly by the clash of ideal and dismal reality, arises this sense of divided personality, the ominous wraith. The terror of his own "St. Agnes of Intercession" of earlier years ironically finds a personal application.

III *Beatrice into Circe*

In 1869 Rossetti was to write another prose piece that like his "St. Agnes of Intercession" of 1850 presented the *doppelganger* theme. The selection is "The Orchard Pit," an argument for a poem which he never completed. The prose narrative begins, ". . . all my life I have dreamt one dream alone." The nightmarish dream is of a glen, a grove of apple trees; in the fork of one tree sits a golden-haired woman who holds out an apple and sings, "Come to Love, Come to Life, Come to Death." Beneath her feet, in a deep pit, partly screened, lie the heaped bodies of her past lovers. The narrator knows that there he too must some day die. The portion of the unfinished poem that was to develop this prose story records the vision of the beloved who draws him to his death:

> . . . her hair
> Crosses my lips and draws my burning breath;
> Her song spreads golden wings upon the air,
> Life's eyes are gleaming from her forehead fair,
> And from her breasts the ravishing eyes of Death.

It is interesting and revealing that by 1869 Rossetti sees in the image of Love, this Coleridgean Christabel, the promise of Death; but the death is not that of "Bridal Birth," written also in 1869, the "nuptial change" that promises the halo of Love's hair. In "The Orchard Pit" Death is a grotesque vision. The name of Death from the mouth of Love, Rossetti writes, ". . . was the very swoon of all sweetest things that be . . . she stood over against me in the fork of the tree I knew so well, blazing now like a lamp beneath the moon. And one kiss I had of her mouth, as I took the apple from her hand . . . I felt my crashing fall through the tangled boughs beneath her feet, and saw the dead white faces that welcomed me in the pit." The bright-haired beloved of "Beata Beatrix," the promise of life through love, becomes the siren figure wooing man to nightmare and to final oblivion.

Two other prose selections of the same period, 1869–1870, *The Doom of the Sirens* and "The Philtre," also reveal Rossetti's growing absorption with the concept of the beloved, not as a source of life and transcendence, but as a damning specter that curses and destroys man. Like "The Orchard Pit," these pieces were never developed as intended; his hopes, for example, for *The Doom of the Sirens* was, as William records later, as a "lyrical tragedy."

As noted earlier, this confusion in the conception of the beloved was observed in his "Dantis Tenebrae" sonnet (1861) on the death of his father, where Rossetti blurs the Beatrice figure from Dante and sees her as keeper of "the vale of magical dark mysteries." This view is partly understandable because of his interest in this period in the Gothic as well as the Dantesque. In his sonnet "Venus Verticordia" (1868) there are also hints of "The Orchard Pit": ". . . if she give the fruit that works her spell . . . /Then shall her bird's strained throat the woe foretell,/And her far seas moan as a single shell."

This poem was one of a number written in 1868–1870 for a series of female portraits, and the list of women is revealing of Rossetti's changing attitude about the symbol of the beloved: Pandora, the siren of "A Sea Spell"; Circe; Cassandra; Helen. When Mario Praz[8] speaks of the cruel, fatal woman in Rossetti's work, he doubtlessly has in mind the figures of this period. The course of Dante Gabriel's thoughts on love may well be mirrored in the evolution of woman's face in his work. From the Virgin in his youthful oil "Ecce Ancilla Domini" to Beatrice of the many Dantesque works; to Guinevere; then to the sensuous faces of Lilith, Monna Vanna, and others; and finally to Pandora, Proserpine, Ligeia Siren, and Astarte Syriaca—these portrayals suggest in his art what lay deep in his troubled mind and in his gradually distorting vision of Love.

With this twisting of the ideal appears the grotesqueness of the female figures themselves. We have only to examine these figures to see the haunting projection of woman—the vampirish depiction of the large lips, lengthened necks, elongated fingers, and haunted eyes of such figures as Pandora and Astarte. The poems he wrote during these years for his oils indicate directly what he intended in these portraits. In his sonnet "A Sea-Spell" (1868), which is a visual development of ideas of "The Orchard Pit" and of *The Doom of the Sirens,* he writes:

> She sinks into her spell: and when full soon
> Her lips move and she soars into her song,
> What creatures of the midmost main shall throng
> In furrowed surf-clouds to the summoning rune;
> Till he, the fated mariner, hears her cry,
> And up her rock, bare-breasted, comes to die?

The music imagery in this sonnet has a new significance, for the music is now the voice of woman who offers madness and death. And, unlike his depiction of Ulysses in his 1870 sonnet "Death's Songsters," who ". . . lashed to his own mast,/There where the sea-flowers screen the charnel-caves,/Beside the sirens' singing island pass'd . . . ," Rossetti feels himself irresistibly drawn; and he asks, as in Sonnet LXXXVII of *The House of Life,* ". . . are songs of Death no heaven to thee?"

Dante Gabriel's general despondent outlook by 1870 is detected in his Sonnet LXXXIII, "Barren Spring." The promise of spring offers no hope for him, "whose life is twin'd/With the dead boughs that winter still must bind." The use of flower imagery in the sestet of this poem may well suggest its use in the female oils of this period:

> Behold, this crocus is a withering flame;
> This snowdrop, snow; this apple-blossom's part
> To breed the fruit that breeds the serpent's art.
> Nay, for these Spring-flowers, turn thy face from them,
> Nor stay till on the year's last lily-stem
> The white cup shrivels round the golden heart.

How often the apple appears in his writings of these years, suggesting deception and death, and perhaps the "fall" from Eden, with Eve-woman the tempter and destroyer of man. In his poem "Love-Lily" of 1869, still voicing the hope that the promise of Love is not a delusion, he writes, concerning the "Eden of Love's watered ways," ". . . let not hope be still distraught,/But find in her its gracious goal."

IV *A Macrocosmic Gloom*

The despair of Rossetti about love spread wide to encompass ultimately his total outlook on life. In his sonnet "The Sun's Shame, I" (1869), he finds most of existence rather meaningless and intolerable: ". . . youth and hope in mockery caught/From life; and mocking pulses that remain/When the soul's death of bodily death is fain." Again in "The Trees of the Garden" he asks of the dead and the living who too shall die whether life has a meaning or is but a mere show, decreed by some inscrutable, relentless power: "is it all a show,/A wisp that laughs upon the wall?" There is no answer from that power that confronts man, "sphinx-faced with unabashed augury."

"The Cloud Confines" of 1871 also raises many of the same anxious questions about man's existence. There is no reply from the dead as to whether there is freedom through Death or only continued bondage. And what of love, Rossetti questions,

> . . . that bleeds in thy breast, O Man?
> Thy kisses snatched 'neath the ban

Of fangs that mock them above;
Thy bells prolonged unto knells,
Thy hope that a breath dispels. . . .

And, as for the man who does ask of the meaning of life, "to him wild shadows are shown."

In the last months of his life, the same despair and questioning concerning meaning in life plagued Rossetti. In his "Michaelangelo's Kiss" of 1881 he writes that "the Soul,/Touching at length some sorely-chastened goal,/Earns oftenest but a little." In April, 1882, when death was near and when Rossetti vainly was trying to complete his unfinished youthful prose tale, "St. Agnes of Intercession," he wrote two mediocre sonnets, still only privately published, on his 1875 pencil sketch "The Question," also called "The Sphinx," drawn at the time of his sketch for the later oil "Astarte Syriaca." Rossetti considered the pencil sketch "a sort of painted Cloud Confines."

In this drawing, one of few art works by him using nude figures, appears a sphinx-like monster, a symbol of the inscrutable mysteries of life and death. While she gazes blindly, three male figures, representing youth, manhood, and old age, climb to her in search of answers. The youth falls back dead, manhood presses forward to ask his questions, and old age toils up the sharp incline farther back. Since one of the primary questions raised in "The Cloud Confines" concerns love, it is appropriate to read into the ghoulish female figure, who draws her victims forward and yields no rewards, the symbol of woman, as in "The Orchard Pit," who first says "Come to Love," and then, "Come to Life," and, finally, "Come to Death." For Rossetti, the soul, touching finally a sorely sought goal, earns but little. The all-important trinity of his *The House of Life*—Love, Life, and Death—remains a maddening question.

As we have frequently noted, Rossetti ends his *House* group, after so many poems of suspicion and despair, with his "The One Hope"; but there remains in it an unanswered question. Beyond death will the soul find "the gift of grace unknown?" Will "the one Hope's one name be there?" Rossetti never says, and his sonnet sequence closes—not so much on the "one sweet, solemn, and joyful chord" as Arthur Benson found,[9] nor even so much on the note of "a sad and resigned Hope" that William Sharp professes to discover.[10] Dante Gabriel perhaps answers his own question six years later in his "Three Shadows":

> I looked and saw your heart
>   In the shadow of your eyes,
> As a seeker sees the gold
>   In the shadow of the stream;
> And I said, "Ah me! What art
>   Should win the immortal prize,
> Whose want must make life cold
>   And Heaven a hollow dream?"

CHAPTER 6

Narrative Poems

IN 1848 Rossetti translated the Italian poet Niccolo Tommaseo's lyric "The Young Girl." Its second stanza reads,

> Yes, it is Love bears up
> My soul on his spread wings,
> Which the days would else chafe out
> With their infinite harassings.

When he sent this piece in 1874 to the *Athenaeum* for consideration, he accompanied it with a letter in which he remarks that the lyric was not "chiefly concerned with public events and interests"; and he refers to the "delicate and romantic tone" of the poem. The Tommaseo poem, although it is a nineteenth-century work, unquestionably rings with the voice of those poets Rossetti was translating in 1847. Placed among selections from Dante Gabriel's (1861) *Early Italian Poets,* Tommaseo's lyric would be almost indistinguishable. In it, as Rossetti remarks in his letter, is to be found the "romantic tone" that he responded to so deeply and so consistently throughout his life.

Besides his translations, other early writings reveal Rossetti's sympathy for this "tone"—his interest in the Gothic past and in the supernatural reflected in his narrative poems and ballads. For a great number of readers, Rossetti has achieved a lasting reputation for these narrative pieces.

I *"Henry the Leper"*

The earliest writing, included by William Rossetti in his brother's complete works, is Dante Gabriel's translation from Burger's ballad "Lenore," the story of a dead man who returns from the grave to carry off his beloved, who awakens to find herself in the arms of Death. In spite of the clumsiness and monotony that some critics find in this early poem by the inexperienced Rossetti, the translation reveals Rossetti's love for the macabre narrative.

In 1846 he translated "Henry the Leper" by the twelfth-century writer Hartmann von Aue. A nobleman, Henry of the Lea, who is handsome, powerful, and rich, is stricken with leprosy. He is told by a leech that the only cure is the sacrifice of a virgin whose heart blood will be his aid. A young maiden offers herself; but, before her death can be accomplished, Henry relents. The inner peace and humility that follow his action precede God's miraculous healing of his leprosy, and Henry marries the young woman. This tale, simply told, reveals early in Rossetti's career his interest in the many facets that ultimately coalesce as part of his peculiar conception of love.

The tale, heavily imbued with religious overtones, brings together a medieval story and the medieval love ideal. What in effect is found in Hartmann von Aue's story is the voice of troubadour poetry: love idealized through suffering, projected through the figure of a saintly woman. Henry and the maid in their final happiness become in part a continuation of the Blessed Damozel and her earthly lover:

> Many a bright and pleasant day
> The twain pursued their steadfast way,
> Till, hand in hand, at length they trod
> Upward to the kingdom of God.

However, unlike "The Blessed Damozel," which suggests much more clearly the implications and the demands of the flesh, this poem remains almost completely spiritual in Rossetti's conception. In fact, Dante Gabriel altered, at a significant place in the poem, a dramatic situation; and in so doing he removed the suggestion of the fleshly from von Aue's story.

In the tale as Rossetti received it, Henry, who hears the leech whetting the knife in preparation for the sacrifice, peers through a crack in the wall to see the young maiden lying naked, bound to a slab. The sight of her beauty decides Henry against her death. Rossetti altered the circumstances so that Henry's decision is made prior to seeing her. R. L. Mégroz explains this change as a result of Rossetti's being then "very much under the Polidori female influence, which was inclined to carry piety and primness beyond the most exalted early Victorian standards."[1] This interpretation may be true, for Dante Gabriel attempted in his early career to keep other possibly disturbing works from his Aunt Charlotte and his mother; however, by this time he had written "The Blessed Damozel."

The portrait of idealized love that Rossetti found in von Aue's story becomes a significant part of his own later love theory, but it is interesting to find in his original work at this time the emergence of the other factor, the role of the flesh, that was to vie with the spiritual and later to so distort that ideal. It is true, however, that, like Keats in the St. Agnes poem, Rossetti in his "The Blessed Damozel" has his most successful portrait of happy love, a love that brings the desired merger of flesh and spirit. But this depiction is challenged in his 1849 translation of the sonnet "In Absence from Becchina," by Cecco Angiolieri:

> I'm better skill'd to frolic on a bed
> Than any man that goes upon two feet;
> And so, when I and certain moneys meet,
> You'll fancy with what joys I shall be fed.
> Meanwhile (alas!) I can but long instead
> To be within her arms held close and sweet
> To whom without reserve and past retreat
> My soul and body and heart are subjected.
> For often, when my mind is all distraught
> With this whereof I make my boast, I pass
> The day in deaths which never seem enough;
> And all my blood within is boiling hot,
> Yet I've less strength than running water has;
> And this shall last as long as I'm in love.

In his introduction to *Dante and His Circle*, Rossetti describes Cecco as the "scamp" among the Dantean poets; and he offers additional observations concerning this thirteenth-century poet that are in a way prophetic of his own life: in reading the sonnets of Cecco, Dante Gabriel writes, "it is impossible not to feel some pity for the indications . . . of self-sought . . . unhappiness, and natural bent to ruin." This "scamp" characteristic is certainly not in Rossetti, except as can be seen in this excerpt from his youthful translation (1847) of a song from Victor Hugo's "Burgraves":

The Devil, hobbling up the stairs,
Comes for me with his ugly throng.
Love on: who cares?
Who cares? Love on.

II *"A Last Confession" and "The Bride's Prelude"*

Rossetti's translations of "Lenore" and of "Henry the Leper" indicate his interest in the narrative poem. His achievement in this genre, seen in such poems as "A Last Confession," "Rose Mary," "Staff and Scrip," "The White Ship," and "The King's Tragedy," places him with Coleridge and Keats in the ballad-narrative tradition. The dramatic monologue "A Last Confession" unfortunately resounds too obviously with the influence of Browning and is not typical of Dante Gabriel's own work. Even so, as a derivative piece, the poem still achieves rather well an engaging sense of the dramatic.

In the narrative Rossetti reveals some of his power of psychological insight. A tortured prisoner reveals to his confessor the sordid, pathetic details of his murder of the woman who rejects him for another after years of his devotion to and sacrifice for her. The poem is as realistic in its details as "The Blessed Damozel" is otherworldly, but these two poems reveal a similar concept in spite of their different handling. In the anguish of his ebbing life, suffering mental as well as physical pain, the speaker hopes that what life has failed to yield will be discovered in death: "May I find you yet/Mine when death wakes?"

The important observation to be made in "A Last Confession" is Rossetti's splendid capacity to tell a story. In this poem Dante Gabriel is able to push on with the facts of his tale while yet building on the picture we have of a tortured and half-mad mind. This interest of Rossetti in the examination of the mind under conditions of stress, often that of a sense of guilt, is found in many of these narrative pieces written throughout his career. And, with this glimpse of the inner thoughts, goes Dante Gabriel's insatiable curiosity in the superstitious and the prophetic.

A great deal of the dramatic interest achieved in his prose selections "Hand and Soul" and "St. Agnes of Intercession" comes from Rossetti's ability to create a sense of internal reflection. And much of the atmosphere of these writings arises out of the pervasive sense of the mysterious. Much that is so important to human concerns is revealed through supernatural means. Sometimes what is revealed is good, as the depiction of Chiaro's soul to himself. This female image becomes the ideal to which Chiaro consecrates himself. Yet again the supernatural may choose to reveal madness and death, often depicted by Rossetti through the wraith or *doppelganger* theme, as in "St. Agnes of Intercession." The use of omen occurs in "A Last Confession." The speaker finds a child, whom he is later in life to love and by whom he is finally betrayed. He brings to the child a gift, a little glass image of Cupid, that holds in his hands a dart and a torch, the same symbols Rossetti later placed in the hands of his "Love" in his sketch "Dantis Amor." The child cherishes the image and places it above her bed; but, as she hangs it on the nail, it falls and is smashed. In falling, the dart that Cupid holds cuts deeply into the child's hand. This incident becomes prophetic of the final tragedy when she is stabbed by the jealous lover.

This interest in the workings of a guilt-ridden mind, revealed in his 1849 "A Last Confession," is better handled in another narrative poem of the same period. In "The Bride's Prelude" Rossetti writes more directly from himself and avoids the encompassing influence of another writer. Rossetti began "The Bride's Prelude" in 1848, then called "Bride Chamber Talk"; and he worked on it again in 1859. Originally Dante Gabriel had intended for the poem to appear in 1849 in the second number of *The Germ*, the Pre-Raphaelite journal; but the tale was never completed. In 1881, when he transferred his *House of Life* poems to his *Ballads and Sonnets* volume, he filled the gap in his *Poems*, which appeared in a new edition then, with "The Bride's Prelude." He had considered the theme of the poem "unelevated and repulsive," and he believed the picturesqueness of the poem was its only quality to recommend it.

Most critics have found the narrative far too ornate, and its profusion of details has been called "Keatsian." Arthur Benson believes that no other poem by Rossetti is "more typical of the Pre-Raphaelite spirit." [2] The tale is of the maid Aloyse, who, as she sits being dressed for her wedding, reveals to her sister, Amelotte, the story of her shame. The experience she relates is about her love and her yielding to the squire Urscelyn. The young man leaves her after Aloyse and her family flee from an attack on the castle. The child of their love is taken from her. Later Urscelyn returns. At this point Rossetti's fragment ends.

A little like his translation of "Henry the Leper," this narrative poem lags; and the main thread of the story is often lost in the detailed descriptions. In spite of this weakness, the descriptions have power. Undoubtedly Rossetti was striving for a projection of the inner mental turmoil into the outward scene. The sense of closeness and of intense and heavy silence that predominates in the poem reflects the enormous feeling of guilt in the mind of Aloyse. Into this scene of tension Rossetti intrudes many sounds that cut unnervingly across the coiled, transfixed silence of Aloyse's room:

> . . . two rooks had toiled
> Home to the nests that crowned
> Ancestral ash-trees. Through the glare
> Beating again, they seemed to tear
> With that thick caw the woof o' the air.

III *"Sister Helen" and "Rose Mary"*

The presentation of mental states, which are often associated by Rossetti with depictions of the weird and the ominous, is successfully handled in his 1851 ballad narrative "Sister Helen." The poem was published in book form in 1857 with some alterations; and, in the 1881 edition of Rossetti's works, the ballad was enlarged. In a letter to Hall Caine, Dante Gabriel explained that a number of additional stanzas were added to treat a new incident in the narrative; and "The gain is immense." The poem has long been considered one of Rossetti's finest works. To a great degree, the powerful impact and ominous tone in the poem are achieved by Rossetti's use of incremental repetition. The refrain of two lines is varied only in the first few words of the second line:

> . . . Three days today, between Hell and Heaven!
> . . . What sound tonight, between Hell and Heaven!
> . . . Lost, lost, all lost, between Hell and Heaven!

As so often in Rossetti's later art, the demoniac woman appears who becomes an instrument of death to the lover. The central figure of the ballad melts the waxen figure of her false lover while her small brother, stationed at a window to watch what may occur, observes the dreadful ritual. In succession the brothers and father of the dying man, Keith of Ewern, come to plead. The most significant addition Rossetti made to the 1881 version of "Sister Helen" was the introduction of the point that Keith has been three days married and of the arrival of his new wife to plead also for his life.[3]

The important change in dramatic handling that Rossetti introduced in his various revisions after 1851 was, however, the projection of Sister Helen herself. Originally the narrative suggested that this witch took fiendish pleasure in torturing her lover. By 1870 her depiction is that of a woman, who, in destroying her lover, also condemns herself. Although the dramatic tempo of the narrative poem is thus increased, Sister Helen, when seen among her later demoniac sisterhood, loses because of Rossetti's change of her supernatural dimensions. It is interesting to note that, in many of Dante Gabriel's early narrative poems treating love relations, the woman often suffers in rejected love; and Rossetti gives the internal depiction of her anguish a psychological realism seldom matched in the poetry of his century. Yet in the *House of Life* poems, the inner turmoil is Rossetti's own. Later, the woman figure emerges as the provocative agent of man's distress; and she finally loses her mortal role and becomes a maddening and destructive force.

One powerful aspect of Rossetti's success in creating dramatic tension in his narrative poems is his sense of point of view: he often places the reader in a position of ironically juxtaposed points of observation which are diametrically opposed. For example, in his early narrative poem "Dennis Shand," a relatively unsuccessful work of 1850 that Rossetti himself did not include in his published works, much of the irony arises from the different understandings between Lady Joan and Earl Simon. His good-natured remarks to his wife upon his return from a journey are sharply contrasted to those of the dissimulating Lady Joan, who conceals her infidelities with Dennis Shand. The introduction of such subtleties as this irony to the ballad format may diminish the vigor of that form, but it certainly increases the dramatic situation in most of Rossetti's narrative pieces. In "The Bride's Prelude" the interplay of Aloyse's guilt with the innocence of Amelotte provides the vivid sense of mental crises that Rossetti was so capable of portraying. In "A Last Confession" there is the growing awareness of the grotesque story related by the rejected lover who awaits execution and seeks absolution from the holy father. His tortured mind is revealed as he tells his story; he approaches the horror of his crime, yet turns away in dismay from the final revelation.

In many of these poems the listener is present; ignorant of what he is about to be told, he must behold the anguish of a tortured conscience: Amelotte hears Aloyse; the priest listens to the half-maddened lover. Each listener has a particular trait, that, in relation to the sin of the speaker, makes all the more intense the other's sense of guilt. In "The Bride's Prelude," it is Amelotte's innocence; in "A Last Confession," the implied priest's spirituality; in "Dennis Shand," the husband's ignorance; in "Sister Helen," the youth and naïveté of the brother. Undisguised evil becomes monstrous in the eyes of unfallen innocence. The reader of the *House of Life* sonnets which touch on Rossetti's own sense of failure should keep in mind such a juxtaposition in point of view.

"Rose Mary" is another of Rossetti's narrative poems dealing with the distress of concealed guilt. The poem was written in 1871 during a period of growing anxiety for Rossetti, after the exhuming of his poems from his wife's grave in 1869, and while he was under the growing power of chloral. The poem, one of Rossetti's longest, was completed at Kelmscott in September, just before the appearance of the Buchanan "Fleshly School" article in the October *Contemporary Review.* During the 1860's Dante Gabriel's interest in spiritualism had increased and this curiosity, at once attracting and yet dismaying Rossetti, appears in such poems as "Rose Mary." The tale concerns a magic beryl-stone,[4] which reveals to the virtuous a faithful view of the future, and to the sinful only a fraudulent counterpart, the reverse of truth. Rose Mary, betrothed to Sir James of Heronhaye and carrying his child, is asked by her mother—who does not know of her daughter's sin—to look into the beryl for a clue concerning the locale of a possible ambush against Sir James. Evil spirits direct the view Rose Mary has, and false information is sent to Sir James, who is slain.

Originally "Rose Mary" did not contain the three beryl-songs that conclude the three parts of the poem. These songs, added by Rossetti in 1879, are chants of the spirits imprisoned in the stone and were employed by Dante Gabriel to weld together the parts of the poem. Supposedly the proofs of the poem were read by Theodore Watts, who believed the poem too difficult for the average reader. After Rossetti had brooded over Watts' judgment, he wrote the songs as necessary links in the hope of clarifying his narrative.

Rossetti had always been interested in the occult. In his very early ballad "Sir Hugh the Heron," written about 1840 and printed only privately in 1843 by his grandfather Polidori, there is the use of scrying. In this tale a knight, away from England during a foreign war, discovers by a vision in a magic mirror that his betrothed is endangered. When Rossetti came to write "Rose Mary" some thirty years later, his interest, encouraged by Henry T. Dunn,[5] shifted from mirrors to beryl-stones. A significant difference here, though, lies, not in the use of the supernatural, but in Dante Gabriel's conception of love in this later tale. His "The Blessed Damozel," 1847, so heavily imbued with the colorings of the medieval and the Dantesque, saw the beloved in the service of Lady Mary. It shall be Mary herself, once hearing of the Damozel's love for her lover, who shall take the two to God. The Damozel, like Beatrice, shares in the splendors of heaven and the light of God.

By 1871, however, with his "Beata Beatrix" behind him, and with many of his *House of Life* sonnets completed, such as "Death-in-Love," Rossetti depicts in "Rose Mary" an awesome alteration. His choice of the protagonist's name is doubtlessly linked with the Virgin Mary, as was the Damozel's relationship in his earlier poem. At the end, in the closing stanzas, Rose Mary is granted a place in the "blessed Mary's rose-bower," an allusion to the Dantean reference of the Mystic Rose. Rose Mary has been betrayed in her love and submission to Sir James of Heronhaye. In Part II of the poem the mother discovers her daughter's sin. Later, while Rose Mary is yet overcome by the news of Sir James' death, the mother goes to the corpse and discovers, in a packet letter in the dead man's vest, the secret that he was betrothed to another, Jocelind, the Warden of Holycleugh's sister. As in the ironical situation in "Dennis Shand," Rose Mary, who shatters the beryl and destroys herself, never knows of the other's unfaithfulness. A good beryl spirit speaks to her in death, bidding her to come alone to heaven "for thy bitter love's sake blest." Rose Mary is told,

"Already thy heart remembereth
No more his name thou sought'st in death:
For under all deeps, all heights above,—
So wide the gulf in the midst thereof,—
Are Hell of Treason and Heaven of Love."

The blessedness she has earned shall be a place "lit . . . /With guerdon-fires of the sweet Love-star/Where hearts of steadfast lovers are." Unlike "The Blessed Damozel," this poem depicts an eternity with parted lovers: there the single heart of Beatrice-Rose Mary resides in the "Heaven of Love." The vast gulf that divides Rose Mary from her lover is reminiscent of the gulf that the gaze of the Blessed Damozel hopefully strives to pierce.

The narrative poems that Rossetti wrote, as early as "Bride's Prelude" of 1848, and coming up through his "Rose Mary" of 1871, reflect this continued double interest, first, in the supernatural, related to the theme of love, and, second, in this changing attitude concerning the love relationship itself. His "Bride's Prelude," "A Last Confession," "Dennis Shand," "Sister Helen," and "Rose Mary" treat the subject of betrayal. The narratives "Stratton Water" of 1854 and "Staff and Scrip" of 1851, although they handle the separation theme, suggest none of the infidelity of the other unhappy plots. Two poems written in 1869, "Troy Town" and "Eden Bower," illustrate this alternating interest in Rossetti. Both were written at Penkill at the time Dante Gabriel was writing "The Stream's Secret," "The Orchard Pit," and *The Doom of the Sirens*—works displaying this fluctuation in Rossetti's expression between the joys of love and of remorse, and containing some of the figures that are increasingly to haunt his works: Helen, Lilith, and the Siren.

Browning supposedly suggested the idea to Rossetti for "Troy Town." Helen prays at the shrine of Venus and offers as a gift a cup molded upon her own breast. Venus is pleased; and Cupid, seeing his own shaft within Helen's breast, sends a second arrow into the heart of Paris. The poem is slight in substance, but it reveals that impeccable power that Rossetti often bestows upon his narrative pieces. Like others of his ballad-like poems, "Troy Town" gains part of its exquisite beauty through the use of repeated end lines, as in "O Troy's down, / Tall Troy's on fire!" The successful creation in the poem of a beautiful sensual mood makes the work one of Rossetti's finest lyrical expressions. Here there is no suggestion of the medieval or Dantesque as in "The Blessed Damozel." The poem becomes an accomplishment of pagan eroticism, an echo of such *House of Life* sonnets as "The Kiss," "Nuptial Sleep," and "Love-Sweetness."

IV *The "Fatal Woman"*

"Eden Bower" is another matter, an echo of another tone, that which is akin to "Orchard Pit" and "Sister Helen." The dichotomy of "Rose Mary"—the "Hell of Treason" and the "Heaven of Love" —is here mingled:

> Lilith stood on the skirts of Eden;
> (Alas the hour!)
> She was the first that thence was driven;
> With her was hell and with Eve was heaven.

Rossetti long had an interest in the Lilith legend, one stimulated early by his romantic reading. His painting of Lady Lilith was completed in 1864 from the model Fanny Cornforth, who figures so often in his sensuous female and flowers portraits. In 1866 he did fragmentary translations of lines on Lilith from Goethe's *Faust*, and the ideas in the following quotation carry over into Rossetti's 1867 *House of Life* sonnet "Body's Beauty":

> Hold thou thy heart against her shining hair,
> If, by thy fate, she spread it once for thee;
> For, when she sets a young man in that snare,
> So twines she him he never may be free.

Dante Gabriel gave an enormous amount of labor to "Eden Bower," a poem about the wife of Adam before the creation of Eve. After her expulsion from Eden and her view of the happiness of Adam and the new Eve, Lilith is driven to seek a mad revenge. She offers the serpent her lasting love if he will join her in her plans to tempt the happy pair to their transgression. Again the revenge motif from "Sister Helen" is used. In this later "Eden Bower," however, the female figure is not humanized; and, with the implications of the poem expanded far beyond those in "Sister Helen" because of the use of the Adam and Eve myth, the Lilith figure, unlike Sister Helen, becomes Rossetti's universalized "fatal woman."

Rossetti's conception of Lilith is not completely successful. Unlike Keats, who made a choice and wrote a successful poem in "Lamia," Dante Gabriel seemingly could not decide between her as a figure of sensuality or as one of demoniac repulsion. The depiction of Sister Helen is clearer; for she, as a force of hate, destroys the lover, although she too perishes in her anguished love. The speaker of "A Last Confession," a completely human characterization, portrays the same role; both he and Sister Helen are lost souls, unlike Rose Mary. One fault in "Eden Bower" is that the narrative thread is blurred in the projection of Lilith's characterization; it is, therefore, unlike "A Last Confession" which is more successful in handling a similar approach. Much the same weakness occurs in "The Bride's Prelude." Where Rossetti's focus is on his story, the poem moves along quickly; and the end result is engaging and successful, as is true of "Rose Mary."

Lilith, as a depiction of the "fatal woman" in Rossetti's work, is found almost everywhere in Dante Gabriel's later expression. She is the voice of "The Orchard Pit" that draws man through love to death. In the sonnet "A Sea-Spell" Rossetti writes that "Her lute hangs shadowed in the apple-tree." She becomes the destroyer of Eden. Woman as the embodiment of love for Rossetti doubtlessly was seen in her inevitable double role. Dante Gabriel might project into her significance the hopeful promise of heaven, but awesomely she could change before his eyes; the Beatrice could erupt into the grotesque figure of "The Orchard Pit."

In his prose synopsis of "The Orchard Pit," composed when he wrote "Eden Bower," Rossetti confuses the woman image. He writes, ". . . I walked with my love by that place and she would needs have me sit with her under the apple-tree in which the Siren is said to stand. Then she stood in the hollow fork of the tree, and plucked the apple, and stretched it to me and would have sung." Although this beloved may later implore the lover not to heed the Siren's song, the apple has been offered from her own hand. Once the heart has touched her shining hair, as Dante Gabriel translated Goethe's lines, the man is hopelessly caught in that snare.

In an earlier episode in "The Orchard Pit" the beloved had offered to the lover an apple, ". . . and as I took it she laughed, and said, 'Do not eat, it is the fruit of the Siren's dell.' And I laughed and ate: and at the heart of the apple was a red stain like a woman's mouth; and as I bit it I could feel a kiss upon my lips." In "Eden Bower" the serpent Lilith extends the apple through Eve. Thus, the fall from Eden for Adam-Man is the work of one woman, Eve-Lilith. The fatal kiss lies at the center of that apple; and the woman's song of love becomes, too late, the anthem of death. The kiss of passion becomes one of maddened destruction. The music has not changed; only man's discovery in it.

In "The Stream's Secret," written at Penkill at this same time, Rossetti discovers that the actual secret from the water is not love, but death. Again the imagery of lips, the promise of love's pleasure, becomes the means of death:

> On deathlier airs the hour must come
> Which to my heart, my love, shall call me home.
> Between the lips of the low cave
> Against that night the lapping waters lave,
> And the dark lips are dumb.

Then, as Rossetti concludes "The Stream's Secret," Love becomes Death, offering the water in his hand. The "Willowwood" poems also of 1869 present the same idea. The ripples of the woodside well "Spread to waving hair," and the beloved's lips rise from out the dark water. When the lover at last drinks from those waters, the hair imagery of his Lilith poem appears again. In Rossetti's prose statement of a never-written poem "The Philtre" the ambivalent reaction of man to love again is suggested. The woman becomes the provoker of love in her lover, then emerges as his instrument of destruction. He dies; and, as he does, "he yields his last breath in a kiss"; but the woman knows "that his spirit now hates her."

In the proposed second scene, Act I, of his *The Doom of the Sirens,* Dante Gabriel evidently conceived of a similar dramatic situation of man torn between the two aspects of love: the true and sustaining one, characterized in the Christian wife; and the pagan and destructive love, represented in the siren Ligeia. The action of this scene of *The Doom of the Sirens* involves a Christian prince, who has been warned by a holy father to avoid the Siren's Rock on his flight with his family from persecution. Instead, he passes the Rock and succumbs to the Siren Ligeia: ". . . the Prince clinging to Ligeia, rapt by her spells into the belief that it is the time of his first love. . . . At last he dies in her arms . . . calling her as he dies by his wife's name, and shrinking from his wife without recognition."

As we have already noted, the state of Rossetti's mind in this period of 1869–1871 was indeed distraught. William Rossetti records, and tries to discount, William B. Scott's account in his *Autobiographical Notes* of Dante Gabriel's impulse towards suicide at Penkill Castle in 1869. Standing above the black whirlpool, "The Devil's Punchbowl," near the castle, Rossetti frightened his companions with what appeared to them to be an inclination to leap over the precipice. A few days later while taking a walk with Scott, Rossetti had the experience of a chaffinch's suddenly settling on his hand. Scott reports that Rossetti believed the bird to be the spirit of Lizzie, returning to foretell some evil; for it was while Rossetti was at Penkill that the recovery of his manuscript from Lizzie's grave at Highgate Cemetery was to be completed. The grotesque task was not carried out by Charles A. Howell for Rossetti until October when Dante Gabriel was back in London. The memories of her continued to haunt Rossetti; and it is conceivable that her power over him from another world, with all its implications of the supernatural, encouraged somewhat the sense of doom and of the fatal woman in his expression of this period.

V *A Change of Expression*

If we accept the principle that an artist may handle a number of themes, but that his chief expressions and more important works tend to gather about a single complex of ideas, then it is interesting to note how an artist may move about that central point. Keats developed slowly during his short writing career, piecing together his philosophic position as he went, but always working toward a primary conception. In such an artist a consistent line of development and maturation can often be traced as his creativity draws about a persistent body of thought.

But in other artists another pattern may be true. What is primary and significant in their work may develop early; and—for various, and often unknown, reasons—later expressions may move away from their point of finest statement. Much has been said, for example, about the supposed "decline" in Wordsworth's poetry, but some sympathetic critics argue that no such loss occurs. Nonetheless, the later poems of Wordsworth do develop another path of ideas, moving out from the high point of stimulation received from his contact with Nature. Whether his Intimations Ode is a farewell or an arrival, a loss or a new gain, is not finally resolved. But what is clear is that what had before prompted his vision, as well as his voice, is now altered. The later poems are less inspired and are not part of his important core of ideas. The earlier voice of subjective expression, drawing directly on the power and vitality of Nature, becomes the more objective speech of a poet concerned with issues outside himself.

Rossetti, after the years 1869–1871, also moves away from his central artistic position. Poems which expressed those ideas most intimate to him, mostly the *House of Life* sonnets and some of his narrative poems which develop about the topic of love, are replaced by two narrative poems, "The White Ship" and "The King's Tragedy," both of which are an imaginative development of historical events; by a number of sonnets on famous personages, particularly the Romantic poets; by a few sonnets on his own paintings or those of other artists; and by several "occasional" pieces. Some of these later poems are good, especially the two narrative poems; but all of them are alien in varying degrees to Rossetti's main body of important poetic statement. These poems, which issue from Rossetti's objective point of view, are poems of evaluation and some splendidly told stories. The few love poems of these years of decline in Rossetti's life are reworked echoes of an earlier passion.

The historical narrative poem "The White Ship" was composed, as William Rossetti notes,[6] mostly in 1880. William indicates that the details of the poem were gathered by Dante Gabriel from historical sources. Rossetti's careful interest in working on his narrative poems of 1880–1881 was prompted in part by a return of health, which enabled him to enjoy a revival of intellectual interests. In a letter to his mother in April, 1880, Dante Gabriel writes that his brother, William, believed "The White Ship" was one of his "very best things." Such a view is indicative of the predominant literary judgment of his day, from his brother as well as from others, that these later narrative-ballad poems were the finest of Dante Gabriel's work.

The poem is based on the tragic sinking of the *White Ship* in November, 1120, carrying from France the son, daughter, and royal party of Henry I, who had gone to France to claim the Norman allegiance. The story is told by Rossetti through the point of view of "the butcher of Rouen, poor Berold," the only survivor. Using this character as narrator, Rossetti is able to gain a great deal of simplicity in the poem; as such, "The White Ship" is perhaps the closest, other than "Stratton Water," to the true ballad style. The refrain, beginning "By none but me can the tale be told," unlike usual ballad form in being repeated at the close of each stanza as Dante Gabriel does in "Sister Helen," is here repeated in three key positions and with great effectiveness: at the outset and close of the poem and at midpoint with the death of the prince. Part of the dramatic impact is achieved by Rossetti, as in his other narrative pieces, through the pervasive sense of irony in the poem. Not only is the simple butcher spared while many royal voyagers die, but the tragedy of the royal party is seen and recorded through his view and speech. Rossetti gives particular tragic significance to the central event through the butcher's presentation, which is one of great understatement. There is a genuine sense of the actual, of reality of human life, that is achieved in the poem through this use of such a candid speaker.

That Rossetti often produces memorable lines in a language of utter simplicity is to be found in the heightened dramatic sense of many *House of Life* sonnets; also in "The White Ship" lines of lasting impact are delivered in unpretentious language. Berold, the butcher, describes the ship's striking the reef:

> The ship was eager and sucked athirst,
> By the stealthy stab of the sharp reef pierc'd:
> . . . .
> And what were men and what was a ship
> Were toys and splinters in the sea's grip.

Part of the narrative interest turns on the fact that the prince, a young man of eighteen who had thus far lived a dissipated, dishonorable existence, dies like a man of true character when he returns to save his sister. Berold records the moment simply: "He was a Prince of lust and pride;/He showed no grace till the hour he died."

The inscrutability of life, so long an aggravating and severe question for Rossetti himself, is partly resolved in Berold's simple outlook. What once was powerful and self-centered is now reduced to nothing by God, for "The sea hath no King but God alone." Rossetti never reached a resolution to his problem of human existence, but a possible answer is offered through Berold. Speaking of the prince, the butcher of Rouen refers to his death: "When he should be King, he oft would vow,/He'd yoke the peasant to his own plough./O'er him the ships score their furrows now."

Although "The White Ship" is not part of Rossetti's love poetry —we are told the poem was written for the children of William Rossetti—there is to some degree a lingering sense here in the narrative of Rossetti's strong inclination toward the supernatural. The poem is far removed from Coleridge's "The Ancient Mariner," both by intention and development; but there are suggestions of that more complex poem in Rossetti's interest in the unconscious world of dream-like illusion. As Berold slips down into the sea, visions of life flash before him—scenes of Harfleur strand, of mothers calling children home, and of the great bells of Rouen. Here the dramatic instance is a reminiscence from the *House of Life* sonnet "The Soul's Sphere," but in the earlier poem the reference has far more ominous meaning: "Wild pageant of the accumulated past/That clangs and flashes for a drowning man."

When Berold rises to the surface of the sea after his frightening "moment's trance" beneath the waves, the sea seems to him a dream. Where moments before there was life, with ship and confusion, there now is silence: "The ship was gone and the crowd was gone,/And the deep shuddered and the moon shone." He finds himself adrift with a nobleman's son, and in the strange solitude ". . . every still star overhead/Seemed an eye that knew we were but dead." Soon the captain appears briefly, learns of the prince's death, and sinks away mysteriously. Then the knight's son is gone, and Berold drifts alone. Fortunately for him, "At last the morning rose on the sea/Like an angel's wing that beat tow'rds me"; and the butcher is saved.

Like the Mariner, Berold must keep his story of single survival to himself: ". . . I told my tale to a priest,/Who charged me, till the shrift were releas'd,/That I should keep it in mine own breast." The poem ends with the refrain with which it began; we hear Berold's voice saying finally,

By none but me can the tale be told,
The butcher of Rouen, poor Berold.
(Lands are swayed by a King on a throne.)
'Twas a royal train put forth to sea,
Yet the tale can be told by none but me.
(The sea hath no King but God alone.)

This voice of humility and acceptance earns from God a survival and yet an implied obligation that must await the release of the shrift. In its own fashion "The White Ship" achieves a dramatic power comparable to that of "A Last Confession," but the involvement of man is far more universal than that of "A Last Confession," which concerns betrayed love. Although "The White Ship" is not of the main body of Rossetti's poetry, it does, like others of his late work, achieve a wider scope of significance in its objectivity. The world of *The House of Life* is close and often turbid; in "The White Ship" the concerns of the human heart transcend personal passion and egocentric vision.

Perhaps Rossetti respected Coleridge for his sense of the universal; for Rossetti writes in his 1880 sonnet "Samuel Taylor Coleridge": "His Soul fared forth . . . /To feed his soul-brood hungering in the nest;/ . . . Richly blest/From Heaven their growth, whose food was Human Love." Rossetti also found in Coleridge the same response to the supernatural and weird that he experienced himself, but he saw in the Romantic writer a "sense of the *momentous*" that he himself spoke of in 1880 in his own introductory *House of Life* sonnet. Doubtlessly this "momentous" sense was related to life in a broad and significant way. The "Human Love" that Dante Gabriel observes in the sonnet on Coleridge as the food of Coleridge's "soul-brood" is of a more profound meaning than the Love that is sought in "The One Hope." In a few of these last works by Rossetti, however, there are hints that "Human Love" may be a motivating force for him.

In a letter to his friend Theodore Watts in March, 1881, Rossetti writes, concerning his poem "The King's Tragedy": "I'm sure I've made the ballad a ripper." The poem has long been a favorite from his works. In the spring of 1881 Dante Gabriel hoped to publish "Rose Mary," "The White Ship," and "The King's Tragedy" in a new volume. As discussed earlier, with some shifting of old poems from his 1870 *Poems,* Rossetti was able to bring out later in 1881 his *Ballads and Sonnets,* plus a new edition of *Poems.*

Rossetti, who had a special interest in Scottish history, particularly admired the famous poem by James I of Scotland, "The King's Quair," parts of which were employed in Rossetti's ballad. "The King's Tragedy," often called by Rossetti "Kate Barlass," concerns the murder at Perth of James I in February, 1437. The incident was probably suggested to him as a subject for poetry in 1869 when Dante Gabriel read "The King's Quair" while staying at Penkill Castle in Ayrshire, where Bell Scott was busy completing murals based on the poem. "The King's Quair" doubtless appealed to Rossetti because of its clear echoes from the troubadour love poems and its strange intermingling of the ominous. Rossetti's later comment to Hall Caine, concerning the writing of his poem—"It was as though my own life ebbed out of it"—reveals the high enthusiasm he brought to its creation.

Walter Pater remarks in his 1883 essay on Rossetti about "The King's Tragedy" that, ". . . if one had to name a single composition of his to readers desiring to make acquaintance with him for the first time, one would select: *The King's Tragedy*—that poem so moving, so popularly dramatic, and lifelike." Although Pater's judgment of this means of experiencing Rossetti's work may be questioned today, the evaluation of the dramatic quality of "The King's Tragedy" remains sound. As in "The White Ship," Dante Gabriel again chooses as narrator a person of simple character: Catherine Douglas, who heroically, yet unsuccessfully, attempts to save King James by holding the doors shut to the royal chamber by thrusting her arm through the locks where the bolts had earlier been removed by the assassins.

Essentially, the historical facts are followed by Rossetti; but his primary innovation is the supernatural materials. James decrees that at Christmastide a festival shall be held at the Charterhouse in Perth; and he rides northward with his royal household for that occasion. On the first evening James is stopped near the Scottish Sea by an old hag who warns him of his coming death. Rossetti's great interest in the supernatural and his long concern with the concept of the wraith occur as the woman relates to James, "'O King, thou art come at last;/But thy wraith has haunted the Scottish Sea/To my sight for four years past.'" Four times the apparition of James has appeared to her, each time wrapped in a shroud. The shroud was first about his feet, then at his knees, next at his breast, and at last about his throat. She warns him to turn back or

"The winding-sheet shall have moved once more/And covered thine eyes and mouth." Her voice panics James' horse, frightens the queen, but at last dies away dolorously on the wind from the sea.

James, who chooses God's way, goes on to confirm his determination to follow God's will; and the old hag is left standing immobile against the sky. Catherine, the maid, records for us the significance of this scene:

> As the ship made way, the moon once more
> Sank slow in her rising pall;
> And I thought of the shrouded wraith of the King,
> And I said, "The Heavens know all."

Later, at Perth, following the religious festival, the old woman returns; but she is turned away. The scene of the king's retirement continues the aura of the supernatural:

> And now that all was still through the hall,
> More clearly we heard the rain
> That clamored over against the glass
> And the boughs that beat on the pane.
>
> But the fire was bright in the ingle-nook,
> And through empty space around
> The shadows cast on the arras'd wall
> 'Mid the pictured kings stood sudden and tall
> Like spectres sprung from the ground.

At that moment the old woman's voice once again rises from the night to the king's window to warn him of his coming death; and in the silence that follows, the sounds of the assassins' footfalls are heard.

Rossetti's handling of the culminating events in the tale is masterful and dramatic. Action is swift, rising to the murder itself, then the poem concludes with the story of the Queen's revenge. During the month that follows James' death, the Queen waits in the chapel with the corpse until Catherine brings her news of the capture and death of the murderers:

> And still as I told her day by day
> Her pallor changed to sight,

And the frost grew to a furnace-flame
  That burnt her visage white.
. . . her eyes were a soul on fire.

The basic facts of the story are set into a frame of supernatural details, but the center of the narrative is a love relationship. Rossetti pictures the love between James and his wife as genuine and warm. In the midst of a world of imminent death, heralded by the foreboding voice of an almost inhuman figure, there flourishes a bright relationship. James sings his song of love to his wife while his future murderers look on and listen. Rossetti interpolates, with some changes to fit his ballad meter, James' own poem "The King's Quair." It is in praise of spring, new life, and new love:

Sing with us, Away, Winter, away!
  Come, Summer, the sweet season and sun!
  Awake for shame,—your heaven is won,—
And amorously your heads lift all:
Thank Love, that you to his grace doth call!

The irony, apparent in the opposition of coming events and the king's song to his love, is sharpened by the commentary of Catherine, who, now later recalling James' murder, relates her story. As James sings, Death takes aim; and Catherine says: "And the grinning skull lurked grimly aloof,/And the wings were spread far over the roof/More dark than the winter night." The summer of Love that James sings of is now seen in grotesque contrast to the winter of the actual world. This contrast not only contributes to the impending sense of danger that Rossetti so well creates; it also heightens the intensity of the love that is depicted.

Rossetti's prose piece "The Orchard Pit" was written in 1869 at the time Dante Gabriel became familiar with "The King's Quair" at Penkill. The use of some verses from James' poem in "The King's Tragedy" reveals a connection between Rossetti's two selections. In the song that James sings to the Queen he refers to the pit that lies beneath Fortune's wheel:

"And under the wheel beheld I there
  An ugly Pit as deep as hell,
That to behold I quaked for fear:
  And this I heard, that who therein fell
  Came no more up, tidings to tell. . . ."

How much a part these ideas played in Rossetti's conception of the frightening pit in "The Orchard Pit" cannot, of course, be known.

These last two important poems, "The White Ship" and "The King's Tragedy," are well-handled narratives that deserved the praise that many of Rossetti's day gave them. Rossetti was developing a promising dramatic sense that indicated an increasing objectivity in presenting his ideas. Although these long tales of 1880–1881 do not reflect his interest in the supernatural—as in "The Blessed Damozel," "The One Hope," and other poems—Rossetti continued to value it. His sonnets of these last years to such poets as Chatterton, Keats, Blake, and Shelley indicate his respect for such an idealistic view in others. Dante Gabriel wonders at Shelley's death what "dread veil/Was rent" for one whose "sovereign guide" was "far-darkling Truth." And, as Rossetti may question the validity of his own dream, he wonders if for Shelley "Was the Truth *thy* Truth?" Again in his poem on Chatterton, Dante Gabriel remarks, "The Angel-trodden stair thy soul could trace." In these men Rossetti must have, to some degree, found an identification with himself. In each sonnet there is a suggestion of the tragedy found in the lives of these poets, either in their failure to be recognized or in their personal suffering and neglect in life.

CHAPTER 7

Last Works

THE sonnets on the Romantic poets, as objective and academic as they may be in their conception, still reveal the pervading melancholy of his later years; and the poems he wrote on paintings by other artists share this same mood and focus of idea. In his sonnet "Spring" on the Botticelli painting he asks, first having described the figure in that oil,

> . . . what mystery here is read
> Of homage or of hope? But how command
> Dead Springs to answer? And how question here
> These mummers of that wind-withered New-Year?

I *A Terrible Reality*

There is no answer to these desperate questions from these "mummers" any more than there is a reply from the silent figure in his sketch "The Sphinx." Somehow in his long narrative poems of his later years Rossetti seems, however, to be implying, after so much personal anxiety, that one must not ask, but accept. Berold of "The White Ship" in his simplicity suggests this new realistic view. By the late 1870's the idealized love dream for Rossetti seems almost dead. In 1875 he had written this fragment: "Thou that beyond thy real self dost see/A self ideal, bid thy heart beware." In 1879, again he was to write one of his many fragmentary thoughts: "For the garlands of heaven were all laid by,/And the Daylight sucked at the breasts of a Lie."

In his last published poem, "Spheral Change," written in 1881, the voice of his darker *House of Life* sonnets proclaims his disenchantment with love and with life:

> In this new shade of Death, the show
> Passes me still of form and face;
> Some bent, some gazing as they go,

Some swiftly, some at a dull pace,
Not one that speaks in any case.

Here are the echoes of an earlier poem, "The Portrait" of 1847, a view confirmed in 1881 by bitter experience. The *doppelganger* theme is in 1881 a terrible reality. The vision of the world as an inexplicable dumb show in "Spheral Change" includes the love vision itself:

> If only one might speak!—the one
> Who never waits till I come near;
> But always seated all alone
> As listening to the sunken air,
> Is gone before I come to her.

We may well wonder what the "one" would have looked like had she paused momentarily and turned her face to the pursuing Rossetti. If his late oil paintings provide a clue, she indeed had become by 1880 a grotesque distortion of the Beata Beatrix.

The last four original paintings that Rossetti began include "La Donna della Finestra" (1879), "The Day Dream" (1880), "The Salutation of Beatrice" (1880), and "La Pia" (1881)—all works that respond to earlier sources of inspiration. In them is seen for the last time a resurgence of the Dantean influence, but what had years before generated hope now erupts in a brooding atmosphere of melancholy and distortion. In April, 1879, Dante Gabriel wrote to his mother that he was busy on three pictures, one of which was the "La Donna della Finestra" oil. He remarked that "times are very bad," and he hoped his oils would "somehow bring grist to the mill." [1] In November of the same year he was writing his brother to visit him on a Wednesday for dinner. "Monday and Tuesday I have other visitors, and find it best if possible to bespeak visits separately, so as to avoid solitary evenings as much as possible." [2] These letters to his family reflect some of Rossetti's personal problems: his increasing debts and decreasing commissions, and his growing fear of loneliness.

Through late 1879 Rossetti worked at his "The Day Dream," the beautiful portrait of Mrs. Morris seated in the branches of a sycamore tree. The need of ready cash pressed Rossetti onward, in spite of persistent trouble with his eyes. In the summer of 1880, when the oil was completed, Rossetti feared no buyer would appear; but the portrait was admired by Constantine Ionides, who finally purchased it for his collection. But other commissions, some partly or fully paid for ahead of time, were unfinished; and patrons, such as William Graham, a member of Parliament from Glasgow, and F. R. Leyland, a wealthy shipowner from Liverpool, began to demand satisfaction. Graham had, among others, earlier commissioned the often-worked-at "Found." In 1873 there had been a fuss with Leyland over the purchase of the "La Ghirlandata" oil, when Rossetti had let the portrait of Alexa Wilding go to Graham.

Rossetti had long been contemptuous toward many of his patrons; to him, they were Philistines to be duped and exploited. Critics of Dante Gabriel's art work have observed that this reaction toward these wealthy or influential buyers, along with the ever-increasing debts facing him, was in large part responsible for the lack of growth of integrity in his productions and for the increase of replicas and potboilers. Again writing to his mother in November, 1879, Rossetti reveals the commercial spirit of his artistic endeavors: "I hear there is a decided improvement in trade. Even cotton at Manchester, which seemed the most hopeless, is looking up decidedly. . . . Iron, copper, and coal mines, also on the mend. You may perhaps think this report not much in my line, but I view it as vitally wound up with the picture-market."

Through the summer of 1880 Rossetti worked on the oil "La Pia" and he wrote in December to his mother that the oil was completed. In large part Dante Gabriel's efforts in these months were goaded by the persistent angry demands of patrons for work long promised and, in some instances, long since paid for. Since 1862, following the death of Lizzie, Rossetti had lived at Cheyne Walk, London; and he had become more and more a recluse. The letters increase in which Rossetti comments on his loneliness and his desire to have William or some other of his few close friends to visit. During 1880, in his need to complete promised work and to pay debts, the work of replicas continued. There were copies made of "Dante's Dream," of "Proserpine," of "The Salutation of Beatrice," and even of his "Beata Beatrix."

After a brief period of apparent good health in 1879–1880, Dante Gabriel began, late in 1880, again to fail. During these years, as William records in his *Memoir,*[3] the family took deliberate steps not to leave Dante Gabriel too long unvisited in the solitude of Cheyne Walk. William indicates that, after Dante Gabriel's return in 1874 from Kelmscott, when he was under the influence of chloral, "exaggerated fancies and morbid perturbations" grew; and with these moods came "grievous thought after thought, supposition after supposition of disquiet, and a nightmare of waking dreams."[4]

II *Distorted Images*

Yet, in the midst of diminishing health and a major endeavor in replica work, Rossetti could still respond somewhat to the emotional impetus of the old love ideal. However, plagued with increasing physical and emotional disabilities, Rossetti produced a series of distorted images in the few new oils of these remaining years. Memories of earlier inspiration from Dante encouraged these portraits. From the *Vita Nuova* the story of the "Lady of the Window," present a long time in Rossetti's mind as a suitable subject for an oil, is depicted with Mrs. Morris as the model. In Dante's work, this woman, thought by Rossetti to be Gemma Donati whom Dante later married, looks down on Dante in his grief. In Rossetti's picture the woman is seated in an open window, leaning with crossed arms on the sill. The head, drawn from Mrs. Morris, is modified by the conventions that Dante Gabriel brought to most of his female portraits. But here are the signs of his late work: lips are pronounced; neck is exaggerated in length; hands are with the taut fingers; and the nose is long.

The large "Salutation of Beatrice," begun in 1880, reveals even more the late corruptions of Rossetti's art; for this picture does not resemble Rossetti's earlier designs evolving from the same Dantean source. The lines that this oil illustrates are from the *Vita Nuova:* "My lady looks so gentle and so pure/When yielding salutation by the way." This passage, as the youthful Rossetti translated it in 1848, presents Beatrice in the figure of the love ideal: "She walks with humbleness for her array;/Seeming a creature sent from Heaven to stay/On earth, and show a miracle made sure."

Beatrice in this 1880 oil is shown as descending a street in Florence. She carries a book of devotions as she passes along a path surrounded by roses and jessamine. Behind her, on an elevated terrace, is Dante, seated at a well and overshadowed by the outspread scarlet wings of Love. For all the years of inspiration that Dante, and especially the *Vita Nuova,* had provided Rossetti, this last painting by him that draws upon this source is indeed a bleak comment on the love vision. Despite Rossetti's sincere efforts in this painting, in which he sought from actual photographs sent him from Italy the details of architecture and settings from street views, the oil was never completely finished. William writes in his *Designer and Writer,* "my brother's shaken and failing health passed into the final stages of disease, and he could work no longer upon the canvas" of "Salutation," even though the oil was near completion.[5]

More than any other painting of Rossetti's final years, this last one of Beatrice displays all the defects of his later style. New problems with chloral arose, and in the summer of 1881 he was to write to Theodore Watts that his physical condition was just "short of the absolutely gelatinous." [6] In this state of decline he worked at the "Salutation of Beatrice" oil.

The result may well be described as near-grotesque. Every quality that might effectively depict the wraith concept is here found. Into this atmosphere, which in some details borders the fantastic, intrudes the visual echo of the "Willowwood" poems. In those four 1869 sonnets, ones which tap so deeply the springs of Rossetti's innermost emotions, is found the confusing merger of the love concept and the many strange facets of the supernatural. The personal identity of Rossetti himself found in "Willowwood" becomes in this "Salutation" painting the presentation of the Dante figure. In "Willowwood" Dante Gabriel sat at the well and finally drank of the dark waters while Love hovered above him. In the 1880 painting it is Dante. The implications of the "Willowwood" poems are undoubtedly brought over to this late Beatrice portrait. The flowers of Rossetti's sensuous female portraits are here the accompaniment of the Beatrice figure. What validity the Rose may have in the Beatrice myth is here vitiated in this ominous setting of foreboding figures. To look at the face in "Astarte Syriaca" (1877) is to find the reflection of this last Beatrice, for the body lines and the arm and hand positions are almost identical. The strange coalescence of the Astarte and the Beatrice figures in his 1861 sonnet "Dantis Tenebrae" has become a visual reality.

The last original painting Rossetti undertook was "La Pia." It depicts the story of Pia de Tolomei, wife of Nello della Pietra, told in the fifth canto of the "Purgatorio." Those distortions of the "Salutation" painting are again manifested. Pia is seen sitting bent forward, gazing out over the poisonous Maremma marshes from the citadel where her husband had placed her to die. The canvas is full of the detailed accessories of ravens, clustering ivy, and tolling bell—all symbolic of the death that issues from the surrounding marshlands. The same large lips, elongated neck, and twisted hands appear as in the "Salutation" painting. Marillier reports that this last work indicates Rossetti's loss of color power.[7]

III *The Esthetic Movement*

In this last phase of Rossetti's life, as he sank deeper into physical and emotional exhaustion and as his last work in art and poetry reflected the darkness of his inner self that closed about inspiration and personal vision, Dante Gabriel was emerging in another role. Since the time of his publication of *Poems* in 1870, which had brought him the first important recognition as both poet and artist, a new group of poets had appeared. This Esthetic School recognized in Rossetti their own concern for beauty and their revolt against much of what Victorianism represented. Many young writers, among them Oscar Wilde, Walter Pater, P. B. Marston, Arthur O'Shaughnessy, and Edmund Gosse, looked to Rossetti for inspiration. F. W. H. Myers, in his "Rossetti and the Religion of Beauty" (1885), signals the identification of Dante Gabriel with the impetus behind this new movement. Writing after the exhibition of Rossetti's pictures at Burlington House in February, 1883, Myers states that those paintings are "the visible sign of the admission of a new strain of thought and emotion within the pale of our artistic orthodoxy."[8] Rossetti becomes for Myers a leader in this movement that looks to a Religion of Art, a Worship of Beauty.

However, Rossetti was never actively involved in any movement and especially in the Esthetic one. William Sharp reported that, when he had once asked Rossetti how he would reply to the assertion that he was leader of the "art-for-art's-sake" school, Rossetti's response was "to the effect that the principle of the phrase was two-thirds absolutely correct, and one-third so essentially wrong that it negatived the whole as an aphorism."[9] Rossetti asked only to be permitted to go his own way uninhibited, writing and painting from his personal vision. It is true, however, that his love of beauty and the search for the ultimate gift of eternal love that he sought did unquestionably mark his many expressions with the open signs of revolt.

The challenge that his art and poetry offered is signaled in Buchanan's blatant attack in the "Fleshly School" article and in numerous noisy and morally indignant statements from warm defenders of the Victorian Philistine principles. The only impact such admonishments had on Dante Gabriel was emotional and physical and was not for him strikes against any of his principles. This reaction was unfortunate for Rossetti; for, had he felt the need to construct a new code and had he sought others to follow it, he might have found a way out of the journey to Camelot that R. D. Waller sees in Rossetti's life.

The mantle of the defender of new causes fell on other shoulders, such as Swinburne's. Unlike Dante Gabriel, who "explained" his position in "The Stealthy School" article, Algernon Swinburne, aggressive and explosive by temperament, conducted a bold defense of his own work. He followed the lead of Baudelaire, whose esthetic theories proposed the belief that "poetry cannot, under pain of death and failure, associate itself with knowledge or morality; its object is not truth, its object is itself." This concept became the artistic position of the group of rebels for whom Baudelaire spoke: "art for art's sake." Walter Pater developed these principles of the new art theory and assumed the leadership of the Esthetic Movement. The belief that the artist writes out of his own responses, giving such experiences a form, is shared by Rossetti certainly and is found in such late poems as his "The Sonnet," which introduces his own such responses to those intimate experiences of his inner self, *The House of Life*. Although Pater called Rossetti "the greatest man we have among us," when the two men met Rossetti's reaction to Pater was, according to Theodore Watts, that he "disliked him extremely."

Personal judgment in art can cultivate chaos and degeneracy, and Pater had misgivings that Estheticism might lead to Decadency, which it did with such a figure as Oscar Wilde. The Esthetic Movement in these extreme positions was despised by Rossetti. In 1881 when Rossetti received a copy of Wilde's first volume, *Poems*, he was indifferent; and, in spite of Wilde's admiration of him, Dante Gabriel would not meet him. Although Rossetti was in his own way individualistic, the young Wilde was openly audacious in his dress, behavior, and language. A follower of Pater, he pushed Pater's sober doctrine to excessive display. The new Esthetes arising in Rossetti's last period took much from the Pre-Raphaelites and their love of beauty, but they pushed it toward a more self-indulgent doctrine. They often became a conscious group, visibly weary with their times, posing in moods of languorous sophistication. The *Yellow Book* echoed their voices in the art of Aubrey Beardsley and in the writings of George Moore, Max Beerbohm, and Ernest Dowson.

Especially toward the end of his life, Rossetti did think and talk to some extent about artistic principles. During his relationship with Hall Caine, he often wrote and discussed matters of poetry. But he never developed any body of ideas, although he always indicated, by his own actions, that the artist was not subject to external laws and judgments. The Esthetes may speak warmly of Dante Gabriel's influence, but he never openly claimed any autonomy for art. The measure of separation between him and the new rebels of art is seen clearly in the difference between Dante Gabriel and James McNeill Whistler. Rossetti by his actions implied, as is true of Pre-Raphaelitism in general, a belief in the independence and superiority of the artist. The public, for Rossetti, was largely the one that bought what he created and at handsome prices often manipulated by Rossetti and by various friends and dealers. His poetry and art bespoke his inner thoughts, which on occasion could shock the more touchy aspects of Victorian moralism; and Rossetti was certainly not indifferent to the reverberations from these shocks, as is indicated in his reaction to Buchanan's attack. But Dante Gabriel's gradual, and finally complete, seclusion, in which both he and his art were largely unknown to the public, added to the developing Esthetic concept of the artist as a law unto himself.

The flamboyance of Whistler was prepared for and made possible in large part by such predecessors as Rossetti. Whistler was Continental in attitude and display, and this fact perhaps kept the Anglophile Rossetti at a respectable distance. The two men exchanged little theoretical influence; Whistler referred to Dante Gabriel, not as an artist, but as "a poet and a gentleman." The precept that Ruskin clarified for the Pre-Raphaelites, when they had no clearly stated principles, was to copy nature; the "stern facts" that Ruskin insisted the young Brotherhood was painting were not the realism that Whistler and other Esthetes sought. Whistler followed Gustave Courbet in developing modern subjects in the life of everyday. To the Pre-Raphaelites "stern facts" meant a careful consideration given to details, but they sought often their inspiration from the past and from the wellsprings of literature and history. Rossetti's one attempt at everyday life was "Found."

The real measure of how widely divided in Rossetti's day were Ruskin's estheticism and the new Esthetic concepts practiced by such as Whistler can be seen in the almost inevitable clash between these two men in 1877. By this time Whistler was designating his paintings with such terms as "Symphonies," "Harmonies," and "Nocturnes." Ruskin viewed his "Nocturne in Black and Gold," a depiction of fireworks at night, and wrote in his July 22, 1877, *Fors Clavigera* publication a criticism that brought a suit for libel from Whistler. Two years before at Oxford Ruskin had called Whistler's work "rubbish," but his commentary in July, 1877, was an even stronger judgment of the new Estheticism in art. He insisted that the Grosvenor Gallery should never have admitted works ". . . in which the ill-educated conceit of the artist so nearly approached the aspect of wilful imposture. I have seen, and heard, much of cockney impudence before now; but never expected to hear a coxcomb ask two hundred guineas for flinging a pot of paint in the public's face." [10]

In the legal suit that followed, Whistler was awarded only a farthing for his troubles, but a new era had undoubtedly come in. He had done for artists in general what Rossetti had demonstrated solely for himself—they were identified as a group responsible to themselves. The removal of the artist and his work from the public domain was in large part a defensive reaction for Rossetti. It is true that for him the average man was unsophisticated, and most patrons were impervious to the beauties of the art they purchased; nonetheless, Rossetti shied away from their criticism. For the rebellious Esthetes the public was to be boldly confronted and its hollow pretensions unmasked. The artists in the new group worked to satisfy themselves, as Rossetti had before them; and the public had but to buy their work in appreciative and humbled silence.

CHAPTER 8

Last Words: A Rossetti Estimate

THIS Estheticism, that developed into the later Decadent Movement of such artists as Wilde, came eventually to the firmer hands of James, Yeats, and Conrad. In "The Cutting of an Agate," an essay of 1913, Yeats recalled his earlier impressions of Pre-Raphaelitism. He recounts how he visited the Tate Gallery and stood before the work of Millais and Rossetti:

> I saw these pictures as I had seen pictures of my childhood. I forgot the art criticism of friends and saw wonderful, sad, happy people, moving through the scenery of my dreams. . . . I had learned to think in the midst of the last phase of pre-Raphaelitism and now I had come to pre-Raphaelitism again and rediscovered my earliest thought. . . . I remembered that as a young man . . . I would be content to paint, like Burne-Jones and Morris under Rossetti's rule, the Union at Oxford, to set up there the traditional images most moving to young men while the adventure of uncommitted life can still change all to romance, even though I should know that what I painted must fade from the walls.[1]

Although Yeats was to go his own way, he saw unmistakably his ties with the Pre-Raphaelite group. In the same essay, he notes Rossetti's contribution to his century and to art and poetry in general:

> Painting had to free itself from a classicalism that denied the senses, a domesticity that denied the passions, and poetry from a demagogic system of morals which destroyed the humility, the daily dying of the imagination in the presence of beauty. . . . The turning of Rossetti to religious themes, his dislike of Wordsworth, were but the one impulse, for he more than any other was in reaction against the period of philanthropy and reform that created the pedantic composure of Wordsworth, the rhetoric of Swinburne, the passionless sentiment of Tennyson.

Yeats is speaking of the results of Rossetti's work, not of the impetus behind it. Rossetti had turned away from most of what constituted the creative environment of Victorian literature and art, but he did so not in a "reaction" that suggests conscious revolt. But, having done so, he assisted his followers in developing a new pathway away from what Victorianism had become. It is rather ironical that what might be called a "fresh" outlook in literature found so much of its energy in the close, dark atmosphere of the Pre-Raphaelites.

I *The Egocentric View*

The turning away from the particulars of his own time for Rossetti came, as indicated, not from any confirmed, well-thought-out desire to proselyte. Out of whatever his Italian background may have contributed—unfortunately some critics have made too much of it—and out of his youth in a family that encouraged so much that abetted the individualistic and eccentric, Rossetti turned in upon himself. What he sought to discover and define was not in Ruskin's sense designed to serve society or to find its identity there. The religious idealism of Dante and the romantic estheticism of Keats merge to produce a strange, exotic experience for Rossetti where Beauty, identified with Beatrice-Mary-Love, is somehow also the beauty of Helen-Lilith-flesh. Obviously this merger is one of incompatibles if both are expected to have simultaneous value and credence. And Dante Gabriel's failure to resolve the tug of war that ensued between the two concepts produced some of his finest statements and most of his peculiar phantoms.

What Dante Gabriel had to say, in his poems and on his canvases, was egocentric. This quality is certainly not in itself artistically deleterious, but in Rossetti it produced a narrow range of conception. His expression turned on emotions and ideas that were too self-concerning. Once this capacity is coupled with the emotional ambivalence, and often instability, as in Rossetti's case, the results can be disastrous. The very ideas toward which his capabilities pushed him remained dubious; Dante Gabriel never finally commits himself. He ranges between the paganism of "Nuptial Sleep," "Troy Town," and the more sensuous oils like "Lilith," and the romanticism of "The Blessed Damozel" and pseudo-mysticism of "Hand and Soul" and "Beata Beatrix." Some of his sonnets in *The House of Life*, such as "Soul's Beauty" and "Bridal Birth," come as close as Rossetti ever does to resolving the differences that sharply exist between his "two worlds."

Conceivably what Rossetti needed was exactly what he seemed to be moving toward late in his life—a dramatic objectivity, in which what he had to say was projected through beings outside himself. Aside from the fact that some of his last narrative poems are brilliantly handled, there appears in them a new sense of conceptual balance. The anguish of tone and the dismay of separated visions are quieted in the simplicity of style and in the serenity of view found in "The White Ship" and "The King's Tragedy."

II *The Unaccepted Vision*

But we do not mean to suggest that Rossetti made a mistake as poet and painter in the selection of subject matter. The trouble lies with his personal weaknesses: a final inability to honestly accept the very ideal that he so warmly conceived; and a failure to broaden the scope of meaning in his expressions, both poetic and plastic, to include the macrocosm as we know it. Again there are hints of a new control in the later narrative poems, but whether Rossetti could have triumphed over the general lack of "dramatic sense" of the nineteenth century to write a good play from *The Doom of the Sirens* can only be guessed. The synopsis treats the familiar topic of love, but perhaps Rossetti's old confusion between flesh and spirit would have vitiated for him any possibly new modes of expression in the dramatic form.

This basic problem of inability, or unwillingness, to believe creates most of Rossetti's troubles as artist. The pursuit of esthetic values always imposes upon the artist's attempt at expression an inherent burden: the abstract must be made concrete. The presence of such intangibles in art creates a diffusiveness that can undermine clarity, and particularly so when the artist himself is uncertain about their validity. When such hesitancy to believe occurs, the artist at best can only hint at the concreteness and believability of those values. As successful in some ways as "The Blessed Damozel" is, there remains in this early poem a final vagueness. What achievement is present came out of an imagination yet uncommitted to reality and to its demands. In poetry, when the writer hesitates in his acceptance of those ideas and values he would speak about, the language mirrors his clouded vision and his uncertainty. Usually what is created is a "sense" of what the poet would portray, rather than the actual concretion through poetic devices. For example, in the 1869 Sonnet VIII, "Love's Lovers," of the *House of Life*, Rossetti treats the love theme that is central to all his art. The sestet reads:

> My lady only loves the heart of Love:
> Therefore Love's heart, my lady, hath for thee
> His bower of unimagined flower and tree:
> There kneels he now, and all-anhungered of
> Thine eyes grey-lit in shadowing hair above,
> Seals with thy mouth his immortality.

For readers who are familiar with the ideas and imagery of troubadour poetry, and who are orientated toward the "romantic" temperament, there may be a perceptual "realism" here. To acknowledge a specificity in this poem is also to acknowledge a willingness to accept Romantic suggestiveness as sufficient proof of the actual.

Keats is certainly successful in this kind of poetry. His portrayal, for example, of the consummated love in "Eve of St. Agnes" is communicated through the imagery of flowers and fragrances and is idealized through the language of religion. But Rossetti's imagery is not so public as Keats'. And there is a vagueness in Rossetti that is not in the mature Keats. The line "bower of unimagined flower and tree" is suggestive, but not specific like Keats' "as the rose / Blendeth its odour with the violet"; and Rossetti's general term "immortality" lacks the evocative clarity of Keats' "famish'd pilgrim," "quest," and "silver shrine." Furthermore, Keats' Truth and Beauty are in many ways more difficult to conceptualize clearly in poetry than Rossetti's fleshly love made immortal; but Keats is convinced that "we shall enjoy ourselves here after by having what we called happiness on Earth repeated in a finer tone and so repeated." Rossetti would like to believe, but finally is not certain. The failure to accept unquestioningly his deepest ideal brought these problems of language to his expression, just as it created much of the emotional turmoil in his life.

III *"Fundamental Brainwork"*

Rossetti attempted in a number of ways to compensate in his poetry for what his conviction lacked. One way was simply to state that body is soul and both are God, but this statement is not convincing. Another is to bring to the form of poetry a strength that the ideas lack, and thus arises so much of his later stylistic consciousness and sophistication. Throughout his poetry there is the deliberate craftsmanship found in much of the poetry of his period. Rather ironically, we have a feeling that Rossetti was to find himself repeating the artistic error of his own character Chiaro of "Hand and Soul." Chiaro, we are told, before the vision of his soul reaffirms him to higher ends, "multiplied abstractions, and forgot the beauty and passion of the world."

Hall Caine's report on Rossetti's theory of poetry remains with the reader conscious of Rossetti's style: "Conception . . . Fundamental Brainwork, that is what makes the difference in all art." Often there is in Rossetti's expression a sense of just how things are said, rather than any attempt to make ideas the matter of communicated experience. Efforts at clear delivery of meaning appear secondary to enormous energies devoted to finish and polish. There were sacrifices of sense to sound that came often when Rossetti, as William Rossetti reports, pored over dictionaries for the precise words he wanted. We have the feeling that his attractions to "stunners" in women also became a linguistic consideration. The simplicity, precision, and clarity of Blake's language and that of Yeats are the poetic achievements of men dealing with actuality; their words take on new dimensions. In Rossetti's poetry there is often the presence of the language of Guido Cavalcanti and Guido Guinicelli. If it is true, as the charge has been made, that Rossetti's translation of the *Vita Nuova* tended "to screw Dante's note up a little higher," then this heightened expression appears more clearly in his own work, especially in *The House of Life.*

The extremely self-centered quality of Rossetti's imagination and creativity necessitated as many ties as possible with the actual world to prevent his talents from being weakened and distorted. In the poems and paintings that were prompted by his idealized love vision, there gradually develops a loosening of those ties and a drift toward the grotesque. However, those poems, especially the longer narratives such as "The White Ship," that do reach out to touch more universal chords of identity attain a wider scope of reality. And it is interesting to note how often the more realistic poems, such as "A Last Confession" and "The King's Tragedy," involve the supernatural, the dreamlike, and the romantic.

Into Victorian England, dominated so much by literature and art that reflected the insipidity of the times, Rossetti brought the distant and exotic worlds of the medieval and Gothic. In his work we find not only much that by temperament is Italian, but also much that transcends country, century, and reality itself. To whatever Rossetti wrote, he gave a precision and assurance often unmatched in his period, despite the frequently overwrought quality of his sentiment. The conscious imitative poems, such as "A Last Confession" and "Jenny," display a dramatic insight and strength that rival the best of Browning, upon whom Rossetti modeled these pieces. Even in those Keatsian poems—"Rose Mary," "Staff and Scrip," and "The Bride's Prelude"—in which every rift is often too loaded with ore, Rossetti achieves a clarity of conception and moves swiftly to tell effectively his story. His power and achievement as translator in his *Early Italian Poets* remain unchallenged. In the language and conception of these medieval love poets Rossetti found his voice and nurtured his most significant dreams. His *The House of Life* sequence draws much of its vitality from that distant time. Through all these writings that so often suggest the visionary and hint at the mystical, Rossetti weaves the strange threads of the supernatural and the weird. His art echoes these unique combinations, and the result is definitely Rossetti's own. We might well maintain what Coleridge said of Wordsworth; for, were we to meet any of Dante Gabriel's work, whether painting or poem, while "running wild in the deserts of Arabia, [we] should instantly have screamed out ['Rossetti.']"

Rossetti's poetry and painting provide a vibrant glimpse into the eternal pursuit by man to find Beauty and Love. Although the power and the achievement of his language in the depiction of this pursuit are undeniable, his greater contribution as artist and poet is to those who came after him. Rossetti reawakened the artist to the glories of word and color that had dimmed in the hands of many in his time, but his own poetry and art are limited. Romantic expression, with lyricism at its heart, arises from the self of the poet; but it yields at last to a sense greater than self. Blake insists, as does Keats, that the direction of poet and poetry, and of man, is to the *not-me*. The poet has no identity except as he becomes the forms he creates. Rossetti was always Rossetti, desperately aware of himself.

To say Rossetti's work lacks unity or direction is not entirely true. Such a work as *The House of Life* does coalesce. But where that blending and centrality in great poetry are found at last in the ideas, in Rossetti they are too often matters of form. To Wordsworth, behind the appearance of this world lay a "more deep seclusion" that defied clear understanding and statement, except in an intuitive sense "felt in the blood, and felt along the heart." The awesomeness of "these steep and lofty cliffs" instill a fear that destroys the poet's self and ours, and achieves the *all*. Often in Rossetti the fear never transcends "in the blood" to become what Aristotle found in ancient drama and what Milton presents finally in *Samson Agonistes*. The "sounding cataract" that haunted the young Wordsworth "like a passion" is in Rossetti a source of fear without *katharsis*, and only in the *katharsis* is there the *not-me* where with ". . . an eye made quiet by the power/ Of harmony, and the deep power of joy,/We see into the life of things."

There are moments, superb, hushed, triumphant, in Rossetti, when we sense a "presence that disturbs"; yet there is a final awareness in us that this "presence" is not intuited. And the "presence" never makes all else in the poetical statement meaningful. Unlike Keats, finally, in his late odes, Rossetti never achieves a sense of a transcendental identity that permeates his expression. His work is scattered fragments of often superb and moving insights.

Maturity in the first-rate poet comes in his thought, a body of ideas that often remains essentially unchanged throughout this maturing. Early poems are awkward, more unrealized, sometimes superficial, scattered statements that later are the same in a more successful form and a more integrated sense. Maturity for Dante Gabriel is, in the main, unfortunately a move from lucid, simple form to a complexity that is more erudite as it is less poetical.

To reach this conclusion about Rossetti's work is not to judge the man or his sincerity of effort; it is only to judge the results in his expression. All of his life Dante Gabriel was fascinated by beauty, and especially by that of the face of a woman. Many are the anecdotes told of his dashing away in the midst of other business to see at closer hand the hair or the eyes of some "stunner." Probably no artist has so caught and idealized woman's beauty in such exciting colors as Rossetti. If we read his poetry correctly, and especially the *House of Life* sonnets, that beauty, as attractive as it was to his heightened emotions and to his artist's eye, was not an end in itself. Behind it he believed there lay some knowledge of the mystery which he sought to understand. If there is "mysticism" to be found in his poems and art, it is in this quest to discover.

His art, such as the "Beata Beatrix," achieves generally a greater insight than his poems do into what he conceived to be behind woman's face. Moreover, Rossetti attempted to some extent to find manifest in this world the ideal in the actual—and here the "romantic disaster" occurs. The medieval knight who professes to elevate himself from one level of existence to another by the glance of his lady's eyes is bringing sense to the service of the spirit. But there is always an inherent, and inevitable, temptation —the desire to find that spirit in the world of sense. To Plato, a beautiful object is but a symbol of the supernal Beauty; the earthly and the heavenly loves are not to be identified. Dante understood this necessary separation. However, in the Rousseauistic sense, both are blended. Joseph Joubert says of Rousseau that he "had a voluptuous mind. In his writings the soul is always mingled with the body and never distinct from it." [2] This merger of these two concepts of love becomes an important aspect of Romantic love. The earlier Platonic sense, so closely identified with Catholic views, comes through Dante to Rossetti, who is influenced in his own time by the impact of Rousseau.

As for the man, Rossetti has elicited many and varied evaluations. His frequent responses to patrons and buyers are regrettable. His relationship with John Ruskin is an unhappy one; but it takes two to make an argument. From the testimony of extant records and biography, there is ample evidence of Rossetti's finer and more generous qualities. Since his death in 1882 an enormous quantity of literature has appeared about him—some laudatory, some not so generous. The interested reader is left to judge for himself about this controversial figure. Not nearly so much has appeared in the examination of his work, and often that material is directed to the purpose of explaining the man himself, not the poet-artist. But one thing in common does remain between the biographical and the critical approaches: Rossetti's identity seems finally to elude those who attempt a definitive evaluation; and, as such, we usually find either those who heatedly defend him against frequent harsh judgment, or those who, without much effort, find details that finally identify a "figure" but lose the actual man. Rossetti himself, like much of his writing and art, prompts examination; but he remains an enigma.

Notes and References

Chapter One

1. Helen Rossetti Angeli, *Dante Gabriel Rossetti: His Friends and Enemies* (London, 1949), p. 1.
2. Violet Hunt, *The Wife of Rossetti: Her Life and Death* (London, 1932), p. vii.
3. R. L. Mégroz, *Dante Gabriel Rossetti: Painter Poet of Heaven in Earth* (New York, 1929), p. 73.
4. Rosalie Glynn Grylls, *Portrait of Rossetti* (London, 1964), pp. 235–40.
5. Gale Pedrick, *Life with Rossetti, or No Peacocks Allowed* (London, 1964), p. 3.
6. The first edition of Marillier's book appeared in 1899. The second, which was abridged, appeared in 1901 and is the edition used as reference in this study.

Chapter Two

1. R. D. Waller, *The Rossetti Family: 1824–1854* (Manchester, 1932), p. 207.
2. Oswald Doughty, *A Victorian Romantic: Dante Gabriel Rossetti* (London, 1949), p. 532.
3. William Rossetti, ed., *The Works of Dante Gabriel Rossetti* (London, 1911), pp. 283–84. All further quotes from Rossetti's poetry and prose are taken from this 1911 edition, which carries William Rossetti's final dating.
4. Mégroz, p. 180.
5. *Ibid.*, p. 144.
6. Doughty, p. 131.
7. *Ibid.*, p. 238.
8. Mégroz, pp. 66–67.
9. Holman Hunt, *Pre-Raphaelitism and the Pre-Raphaelite Brotherhood* (New York, 1906), II, 164.
10. Doughty, pp. 263–64.
11. William Rossetti, *Dante Gabriel Rossetti: His Family Letters with a Memoir* (London, 1895), I, 203; hereafter referred to as *Memoir*.

12. Mégroz, p. 76.
13. H. C. Marillier, *Dante Gabriel Rossetti: An Illustrated Memorial of His Art and Life* (London, 1901), pp. 98–99.
14. *Ibid.*, p. 110.
15. George H. Ford, *Keats and the Victorians* (New Haven, 1944), pp. 128–29.
16. William Rossetti, *Dante Gabriel Rossetti as Designer and Writer* (London, 1889), p. 157; hereafter referred to as *Designer and Writer.*
17. *Ibid.*
18. *Ibid.*, p. 160.
19. *Ibid.*, pp. 108–9.
20. Marillier, p. 132.
21. Hall Caine, *Recollections of Rossetti* (London, 1928), pp. 70–71.
22. *Ibid.*, p. 200.
23. William Rossetti, *Designer and Writer*, p. 175.

Chapter Three

1. Waller, p. 129.
2. *Ibid.*, p. 188.
3. William Rossetti, *Designer and Writer*, p. 125.
4. Waller, p. 192.
5. Mégroz, p. 183.
6. William Sharp, *Dante Gabriel Rossetti: A Record and A Study* (London, 1882), p. 310.
7. Joseph Knight, *Life of Dante Gabriel Rossetti* (London, 1887), p. 84.
8. Arthur C. Benson, *Rossetti* (New York, 1904), p. 152.
9. Mégroz, pp. 160–72.
10. Waller, p. 193.
11. William Rossetti, *Memoir*, II, 38.
12. Mario Praz, *The Romantic Agony* (New York, 1956), p. 218.
13. Hunt, I, 154.
14. Waller, p. 205.
15. Mégroz, p. 171.
16. Doughty, p. 477.
17. William Rossetti, *Designer and Writer*, p. 132.
18. Benson, p. 157.
19. Sharp, p. 297.
20. Doughty, p. 264.
21. Ford, p. 123. Ford notes that what Rossetti found in Keats that made Keats for him a well-loved poet was the power of intensity and a "highly finished pictorial power."
22. William Rossetti, *Memoir*, I, 171.

Chapter Four

1. Graham Hough, *The Last Romantics* (London, 1947), p. 67.
2. William Rossetti, *Designer and Writer,* p. 184.
3. Paull F. Baum, ed., *The House of Life: A Sonnet Sequence,* by Dante Gabriel Rossetti (Cambridge, 1928), p. 59.
4. Sharp, p. 44.
5. Caine, p. 112.
6. Benson, p. 74.
7. Sharp, p. 406.
8. Knight, p. 165.
9. William Rossetti, *Designer and Writer,* p. 179.
10. William Rossetti, *Some Reminiscences* (New York, 1906), II, 478.
11. Benson, p. 136.
12. Baum, p. 3.
13. William Rossetti, *Memoir,* I, 420.
14. Knight, p. 28.
15. William Rossetti, ed., *The Collected Works of Dante Gabriel Rossetti* (London, 1897), I, xxxiv.
16. Principal Shairp, "Aesthetic Poetry: Dante Gabriel Rossetti," *Eclectic Magazine,* XCIX (September 1882), 341–51.
17. Benson, pp. 81–84.
18. Baum, pp. 10, 15.
19. Doughty, p. 398.
20. Ford, p. 140.
21. Caroline Spurgeon, *Mysticism in English Literature* (London, 1922), pp. 33–56.
22. F. W. H. Myers, "Rossetti and the Religion of Beauty," *Essays Modern* (London, 1885), pp. 312–34.
23. C. M. Bowra, *The Romantic Imagination* (New York, 1961), pp. 197–220.
24. Hough, p. 80.
25. Mégroz, p. 186.
26. William Rossetti, *Rossetti Papers: 1862–1870* (London, 1903), II, 528–29.
27. Robert Buchanan, "The Fleshly School of Poetry: Dante Gabriel Rossetti," *Notorious Literary Attacks,* ed., Albert Mordell (New York, 1926), p. 203.
28. William Rossetti, *Rossetti Papers,* pp. 455–56.
29. Doughty, p. 384.
30. Mégroz, p. 295.
31. Marillier, p. 49.
32. *Ibid.,* p. 76.

33. Benson, p. 184.
34. Doughty, p. 255.
35. *Ibid.*, p. 684.

Chapter Five

1. William Rossetti, *Designer and Writer*, p. 181.
2. Waller, p. 207.
3. Doughty, p. 122.
4. *Ibid.*, p. 154.
5. William Rossetti, *Memoir*, I, 167.
6. Doughty, p. 134.
7. *Ibid.*, p. 138.
8. Praz, p. 218.
9. Benson, p. 134.
10. Sharp, p. 431.

Chapter Six

1. Mégroz, p. 224.
2. Benson, p. 110.
3. Sharp, pp. 356–61, gives a complete and careful account of these changes in the 1881 edition.
4. Doughty, p. 476, speaks of Rossetti's source in the use of the stone.
5. Henry Treffry Dunn, *Recollections of Dante Gabriel Rossetti and His Circle* (New York, 1904), pp. 62–63.
6. William Rossetti, *Designer and Writer*, p. 170.

Chapter Seven

1. William Rossetti, *Memoir*, II, 351–52.
2. *Ibid.*, p. 354.
3. *Ibid.*, I, 360.
4. *Ibid.*
5. William Rossetti, *Designer and Writer*, p. 110.
6. Doughty, p. 634.
7. Marillier, p. 141.
8. Myers, p. 313.
9. William Rossetti, *Memoir*, I, 413.
10 Horace Gregory, *The World of James McNeill Whistler* (New York, 1959), p. 132.

Chapter Eight

1. W. B. Yeats, *Essays and Introductions* (New York, 1961), pp. 346–47.
2. Irving Babbitt, *Rousseau and Romanticism* (New York, 1957), pp. 175–76.

Selected Bibliography

PRIMARY SOURCES

The most complete edition of Rossetti's work is that edited by his brother, William, *The Works of Dante Gabriel Rossetti* (London: Ellis, 1911). Each poem is dated, and this edition includes a number of pieces appearing in print for the first time, particularly in the sections "Versicles and Fragments," "Juvenilia and Grotesques," and "Prose." Moreover, some selections printed elsewhere but never included in a collected edition are found here.

Other editions by William Rossetti which are worth the reader's attention include the two-volume 1887–1888 collected works; the two-volume 1904 edition, which includes once again the controversial sonnet "Nuptial Sleep," which Rossetti had canceled after the sixth printing of the 1870 *Poems* volume and omitted from the 1881 new edition; and a shorter one-volume edition, 1905, of the poems, which does not include William's usual helpful notes.

A good number of collections of letters are available, a great many edited carefully by William Rossetti. These collections worthy of careful consideration are William's two-volume *Dante Gabriel Rossetti: His Family-Letters with a Memoir* (London: Ellis, 1895). The first volume contains the invaluable memoir; and the second, the letters, 1842–1882, with helpful notes. William Rossetti's collection *Rossetti Papers*, 1862–1870 (London: Sands, 1903), is a supplement to the *Memoir* edition, and includes over three hundred letters to and from William and Dante Gabriel and their friends and associates.

This *Rossetti Papers* was intended by William to continue his collection of letters *Ruskin: Rossetti: Preraphaelitism* (London: George Allen, 1899), which is illuminating in understanding the Rossetti biography, 1854–1862, in that period when he knew Elizabeth Siddal and was befriended by John Ruskin. Two volumes which are important in understanding Rossetti in the early years are the 1900 *Preraphaelite Diaries and Letters*, edited by William Rossetti; and George B. Hill's edition of Rossetti's letters to William Allingham, 1854–1870 (London: T. Fisher Unwin, 1897). Janet Camp Troxell's edition *Three Rossettis* (Cambridge: Harvard University Press, 1937), includes some theretofore unpublished letters to and from Dante Gabriel, Christina, and William. The most recent is a four-volume collection, *Letters, 1835–1882*, edited by Oswald Doughty and J. R. Wahl, perhaps to date the most complete of Rossetti's correspondence.

Other useful small collections of letters to and from Dante Gabriel Rossetti include *The Letters of Dante Gabriel Rossetti to his Publisher, F. S. Ellis,* edited by Oswald Doughty (London: Scholartis Press, 1928); *Dante Gabriel Rossetti: Letters to Miss Alice Boyd,* edited by John Purves, *Fortnightly Review,* May, 1928; *Dante Gabriel Rossetti's Letters to Fanny Cornforth,* edited by Paull Baum (Baltimore: Johns Hopkins University Press, 1940); and, recently, *The Rossetti-Macmillan Letters,* edited by Lona Mosk Packer (Berkeley: University of California Press, 1963).

Individual or collected works not listed above include these:

The Ballad of Jan Van Hunks. London: George G. Harrap Company, Ltd., 1929. (An edition, 1912, ed., T. J. Wise; and in 1952, ed., J. R. Wahl.)

Ballads and Sonnets (Tauchnitz Edition). New York: White, Stokes, and Allen, 1882. (This edition includes a brief memoir by Francis Hueffer.)

Ballads and Sonnets. London: Ellis, 1881.

"The Blessed Damozel." *The Unpublished Manuscript, Texts and Collation.* Ed., Paull F. Baum. Chapel Hill: University of North Carolina Press, 1938.

Burger's "Lenore." Ed., W. M. Ross. London: Ellis, 1900.

The Collected Works of Dante Gabriel Rossetti. Ed., William Michael Rossetti. 2 vols. London: Ellis, 1897.

Dante Gabriel Rossetti: An Analytical List of Manuscripts in Duke University Library with hitherto Unpublished Verse and Prose. Ed., Paull F. Baum. Durham: Duke University Press, 1931.

Dante Gabriel Rossetti: An Anthology. Chosen by F. L. Lucas. Cambridge: Cambridge University Press, 1933.

Dante Gabriel Rossetti: An Illustrated Memorial of His Art and Life Ed., H. C. Marillier. London: George Bell and Sons, 1901. (Contains 103 prints of Rossetti's art.)

Dante Gabriel Rossetti. London: George Newnes, Ltd., n. d. (Edition with 57 plates of Rossetti's art, with an introduction by Ernest Radford.)

Dante Gabriel Rossetti: Poems. Ed., Oswald Doughty. London: J. M. Dent, 1957.

Dante Gabriel Rossetti: Poems and Translations, 1850–1870, together with the Prose Story "Hand and Soul." London: Oxford University Press, 1913.

The Dusseldorf Artists' Album. Ed., Mary Howitt. London: Trubner and Company, 1854. (Facsimile, ed., M. Foerster, Leipzig, 1929.) (Contains "Sister Helen," signed H.H.H.)

The Early Italian Poets, together with Dante's "Vita Nuova." London: Smith, Elder Company, 1861. (Revised and rearranged in 1874 with some new translations as *Dante and His Circle*.)

"The Full Text of Rossetti's Sonnet on Sordello." Ed., R. F. Metzdorf. *Harvard Library Bulletin*, VII (1953).

The Germ: Thoughts toward Nature in Poetry, Literature, and Art. No. 1 and 2, January, February, 1850. (Continued as) *Art and Poetry: Being Thoughts toward Nature, Conducted Principally by Artists*. No. 3 and 4, March, April, 1850. (Nos. 1–4, facsimile reprint by William Rossetti, 1901; facsimile reprint, AMS Press, Inc., New York, 1964.) Works by D. G. Rossetti: in No. 1 appears one poem and one prose tale. In No. 2, one poem; in No. 3, two poems; and in No. 4, eight pieces.)

The House of Life: A Sonnet-Sequence. Ed., P. F. Baum. Cambridge: Harvard University Press, 1928. (This edition includes a prose statement of the sonnets, a very helpful introduction, and work on dating of the sonnets.)

"Of Life, Love and Death: Sixteen Sonnets," *Fortnightly Review*, XI (March, 1869), 266–73.

The Oxford and Cambridge Magazine. Eds., W. Fulford and W. Morris, 1856. (No. 8 contains Rossetti's "The Burden of Nineveh"; No. 11, the second version of "The Blessed Damozel"; and No. 12, "Staff and Scrip.")

Pictures and Poems of Dante Gabriel Rossetti. Arranged by Fitz Roy Carrington. New York: Russell, 1900.

Poems. London: Ellis, 1870. (A new edition, 1881.)

Poems, Ballads and Sonnets. Ed., P. F. Baum. New York, 1937.

Poems by Dante Gabriel Rossetti. New York: John B. Alden, 1885.

Rossetti's "Sister Helen." Ed., Janet Camp Troxell. New Haven: Yale University Press, 1939.

Sir Hugh the Heron: A legendary tale in four parts. London: Privately printed by Gaetano Polidori, 1843.

"Some Unpublished Stanzas by Rossetti." Ed., M. L. Howe, *Modern Language Notes*, XLVIII (1933).

SECONDARY SOURCES

I. *Bibliographical*

BATESON, F. W. *The Cambridge Bibliography of English Literature*. Vol. III, 271–73. New York: The Macmillan Company, 1941. (Vol. V, supplement, 593–94.)

EHRSAM, T. G., R. H. DEILY, and R. M. SMITH. *Bibliographies of Twelve Victorian Authors.* New York: H. W. Wilson Company, 1936. Pp. 201–25.

FREDEMAN, WILLIAM E. *Pre-Raphaelitism: A Bibliocritical Study.* Cambridge: Harvard University Press, 1965.

FUCILLA, J. G. "Bibliographies of Twelve Victorian Authors: A Supplement," *Modern Philology,* XXXVII (1939).

ROSSETTI, WILLIAM M. *Bibliography of the Works of Dante Gabriel Rossetti.* London: Ellis, 1905.

VAUGHAN, CHARLES E. *Bibliography of the Works of Dante Gabriel Rossetti.* Oxford: Horace Hart, 1914. (The English Association pamphlet #29.)

WATSON, GEORGE, ed. *Concise Cambridge Bibliography of English Literature.* Cambridge: Cambridge University Press, 1958.

II. *Critical and Biographical*

ANGELI, HELEN ROSSETTI. *Dante Gabriel Rossetti: His Friends and Enemies.* London: Hamish Hamilton, 1949. Sympathetic defense of Dante Gabriel by William's daughter. She examines Rossetti's friendships with such notables as Holman Hunt, Ruskin, Swinburne, Morris, Meredith, Whistler, and others.

——. *Pre-Raphaelite Twilight: The Story of Charles Augustus Howell.* London: The Richards Press, 1954. A defense of Howell, biased somewhat because of the author's close family feeling. Interesting insight into a figure often condemned in Rossetti studies.

BABBITT, IRVING. *Rousseau and Romanticism.* New York: Meridian Books, 1957. Excellent study for general background understanding of such topics as Romantic Imagination and Romantic Love.

"Ballads and Sonnets," *Harper's Magazine,* LXIV (February 1882), 473. A study of this 1882 edition finds much in "the art of poetic feigning" and artificial emotions.

BATE, PERCY. *The English Pre-Raphaelite Painters.* London: George Bell and Sons, 1905. Early, reliable study of individual members of the PRB and their followers; now followed by current studies such as Lang's, 1968.

BAUM, PAULL F. "Dante Gabriel Rossetti: Poems," *Victorian Studies,* I (December 1957), 203–4. Baum objects to Doughty's 1957 edition of *Poems,* asserting that the *House* sequence is divided, thus disrupting the general movement of the collection.

——. "Two Victorian Poets," *Yale Review,* XXXIV (March 1950), 570–72. Objects to Doughty's biography of Rossetti as too concerned with a parade of facts depicting a case history of a psychotic.

BEERBOHM, MAX. *Rossetti and His Circle.* London: William Heinemann,

1922. Delightful set of twenty-three plates depicting situations in the lives of Rossetti and his associates.

BEHRMAN, S. N. *Conversation with Max.* London: Hamish Hamilton, 1960. Study of Sir Max Beerbohm, who knew at first hand much of the later period of the Esthetic Movement. Some few references to Rossetti.

BENSON, ARTHUR C. *Rossetti.* New York: The Macmillan Company, 1904. Sympathetic early study of Rossetti; examines biography, works, and style.

BICKLEY, FRANCIS. *The Pre-Raphaelite Comedy.* London: Constable and Co., Ltd., 1932. Readable, careful look at Hunt, Millais, and Rossetti in the PRB group.

BOWRA, C. M. *The Romantic Imagination.* New York: Oxford University Press, 1961. Sound chapter on *The House of Life;* sees Rossetti as pursuing the ideal of Beauty.

BOYD, EVELYN M. "Dante Gabriel Rossetti's *House of Life:* A Study of its Italian Background" (dissertation), Columbia University, 1954. Examines the iconography from early Italian poets in the *House* sequence.

BROOKE, STOPFORD A. *Four Victorian Poets.* New York: G. P. Putnam's Sons, 1908. Finds beauty, precision, and finish in Rossetti's poetry, especially in the sonnets.

BUCHANAN, ROBERT. "The Fleshly School of Poetry: Dante Gabriel Rossetti." *Notorious Literary Attacks.* Ed., Albert Mordell. New York: Boni and Liveright, 1926. Convenient collection of well-known critical attacks against significant writers.

BUCKLEY, JEROME H. *The Victorian Temper.* Cambridge: Harvard University Press, 1951. Examines use of conceits between Rossetti and Donne.

CAINE, HALL. *Recollections of Rossetti.* London: Cassell and Company, Ltd., 1928. Firsthand account of Rossetti's last years by a man close to the poet-artist. Must be read with care since Caine is apt to dramatize.

CARY, ELISABETH LUTHER. *The Rossettis: Dante Gabriel and Christina.* New York: G. P. Putnam's Press, 1900. Well-illustrated, readable life; two chapters on Christina.

CECIL, LORD DAVID. "Gabriel Charles Dante Rossetti." *The Great Victorians.* Eds., H. J. and Hugh Massingham. New York: Macmillan Company, 1932. Maintains that Rossetti's style has unity of tone and theme, but is too artificial.

DOUGHTY, OSWALD. *Dante Gabriel Rossetti.* London: Longmans, Green and Company, 1957. Brief, but informative study of Rossetti in the "Writers and Their Works" series.

———. "Rossetti's Conception of the 'Poetic' in Poetry and Painting,"

Essays by Divers Hands, XXVI (1953), 89–103. Sees in Rossetti's work the presence of supramundane, the passionate search for the twin soul.

——. *A Victorian Romantic: Dante Gabriel Rossetti.* London: Frederick Muller, Ltd., 1949. Excellent, full study that remains the best on Rossetti biography.

DUNN, HENRY TREFFRY. *Recollections of Dante Gabriel Rossetti and His Circle.* London: Elkin Matthews, 1904. Personal account by Rossetti's art assistant of almost twenty years at Cheyne Walk.

FAVERTY, FREDERIC E., ed. *The Victorian Poets.* Cambridge: Harvard University Press, 1956. Excellent presentation of research completed and suggestions for further study among major Victorian poets.

FORD, GEORGE H. *Keats and the Victorians.* New Haven: Yale University Press, 1944. Traces some of the verbal and thematic influences from Keats.

FOSTER, NANCY K. "A Word for Rossetti," *Poet-Lore,* XXI (July, 1910), 322–29. Sees mysticism in Rossetti's work and a superiority over Shakespeare's sonnets in delicacy and mystery.

GAUNT, WILLIAM. *The Pre-Raphaelite Tragedy.* New York: Harcourt, Brace and Company, 1942. Very readable account of the PRB group, its failures of personal ambitions and the gradual decline in Rossetti's visions.

GRAY, NICOLETTE. *Rossetti, Dante and Ourselves.* London: Faber and Faber, 1947. Examination of influences from Dante.

GREGORY, HORACE. *The World of James McNeill Whistler.* New York: Thomas Nelson and Sons, 1959. Illuminates the relations of Whistler and Rossetti in years following Lizzie's death.

GRIERSON, H. J. C. *Lyrical Poetry of the Nineteenth Century.* New York: Harcourt, Brace and Company, 1929. Sees source of Rossetti's Romantic inspiration in German poetry.

GRYLLS, ROSALIE GLYNN. *Portrait of Rossetti.* London: Macdonald, 1964. Sympathetic reassessment of Rossetti's life; includes the recently released letters between Rossetti and Mrs. Morris, plus other newly published materials and illustrations.

HAMILTON, G. R. "Dante Gabriel Rossetti," *Criterion,* VII (June 1928), 91–103. Maintains that Rossetti's abundant sense of the "ritual of the body" dims any spiritual perception. Occasional sublimation of the senses never permits a mystic illumination.

HEATH-STUBBS, JOHN. *The Darkling Plain.* London: Eyre and Spottiswoode, 1950. Good study of connections between the Pre-Raphaelite group and the Esthetic Movement.

HELLINGS, EMMA L. "Rossetti's Treatment of Love," *Poet-Lore,* XVI (Spring 1905), 76–79. Sees in Rossetti's vision of Love the perfect communion of body and soul, providing the moment of mystic insight.

HOUGH, GRAHAM. *The Last Romantics.* London: Methuen, 1947. Excellent chapter on the Pre-Raphaelite esthetic and on Rossetti's poetry.

HUEFFER, FORD MADOX. *Ancient Lights and Certain New Reflections.* London: Chapman and Hall, Ltd., 1911. Helen Rossetti Angeli takes Hueffer to task (1949) for the inaccuracies of his volume.

HUNT, VIOLET. *The Wife of Rossetti: Her Life and Death.* London: John Lane Ltd., 1932. Generally established now as too sensational and suspect.

HUNT, W. HOLMAN. *Pre-Raphaelitism and the Pre-Raphaelite Brotherhood.* 2 vols. New York: Macmillan and Company, 1906. Full account of the Brotherhood by one of its chief participants, who, long loyal to its tenets, tries to play down some of Rossetti's importance as leader.

KNICKERBOCKER, K. L. "Rossetti's 'The Blessed Damozel,'" *Studies in Philology,* XXIX (1932), 485–504. Worthwhile study of the literary influences on this poem, and of revisions which reveal the poem was not fully realized in Rossetti's youth as some critics state.

KNIGHT, JOSEPH. *Life of Dante Gabriel Rossetti.* London: Walter Scott, 1887. Early eulogistic study of Rossetti's life and work by an old friend.

KUHNS, OSCAR. *Dante and the English Poets from Chaucer to Tennyson.* New York: Henry Holt, 1904. Early, sketchy consideration of Dante in Rossetti's work, especially in his paintings. Only hints at Dantean influence in the poetry.

LANG, CECIL Y., ed. *The Pre-Raphaelites and Their Circle.* Boston: Houghton Mifflin Company, 1968. Good introduction, and some plates of Pre-Raphaelite art.

LITTELL, PHILIP. "Books and Things," *New Republic,* XXVII (June 15, 1921), 84. Sympathetic look at Rossetti's style and language.

LUCAS, F. L. *Victorian Poets.* London: Cambridge University Press, 1940. Readable, general introductions to Tennyson, Browning, Patmore, the Rossettis, and others.

MARILLIER, H. C. *Dante Gabriel Rossetti: An Illustrated Memorial of His Art and Life.* London: George Bell and Sons, 1901. Beautifully illustrated study of Rossetti's art; still respected and most valuable.

MASEFIELD, JOHN. *Thanks Before Going.* New York: Macmillan, 1947. Appreciative study of Rossetti's style and subject in his sonnets.

MÉGROZ, R. L. *Dante Gabriel Rossetti: Painter Poet of Heaven in Earth.* New York: Charles Scribner's Sons, 1929. One of the first genuine attempts to study Rossetti's ideas and concepts and still a most helpful volume.

MYERS, F. W. H. *Essays, Modern.* London: Macmillan and Company, 1885. Early interesting examination of Rossetti in the "Religion of Beauty."

PEDRICK, GALE. *Life with Rossetti, or No Peacocks Allowed.* London: Macdonald, 1964. Interesting examination of Dunn, who spent so many years in close association with Rossetti at Cheyne Walk.

"The Poems of Dante Gabriel Rossetti," *Eclectic Magazine,* LXXV (August 1870), 143–54. Discovers little of poetic stature in Rossetti's works.

"The Poetry of Rossetti," *British Quarterly Review,* LXXVI (July 1882), 109–27. An unfriendly review of Rossetti's poems, concentrating on ornate style and sensuality of treatment.

PRAZ, MARIO. *The Flaming Heart.* New York: Doubleday and Company, 1958. Sees some relationship in handling of language between Rossetti and Marino.

——. *The Romantic Agony.* New York: Meridian Books, 1956. Provocative look at Rossetti's projection of female figures in his work.

PRESTON, KERRISON. *Blake and Rossetti.* London: Alexander Moring Ltd., 1944. Significant comparison of the ideas and work of these two poet-artists.

RADFORD, ERNEST. *Dante Gabriel Rossetti.* London: George Newnes Ltd., n. d. Collection of fifty-seven prints of Rossetti's art with a brief introductory discussion about this work.

ROSENBAUM, ROBERT A. *Earnest Victorians.* New York: Hawthorn Books, 1961. Glimpse of Rossetti in the Pre-Raphaelite years, taken from diaries, letters, and biographies of associates.

"Rossetti and the Moralists," *Fortnightly Review,* LV (March 1891), 406–12. Finds "hot house" atmosphere and overworked style in Rossetti's poetry.

ROSSETTI, WILLIAM MICHAEL. *Dante Gabriel Rossetti as Designer and Writer.* London: Cassell and Company, Ltd., 1889. Important observations of *House of Life,* with a paraphrase of those sonnets.

——. *Some Reminiscences.* 2 vols. New York: Charles Scribner's Sons, 1906. Pertinent, interesting insights into Rossetti family and relations with friends.

"Rossetti's Poems," *Edinburgh Review,* CLV (April 1882), 322–37. Caustic review maintaining Rossetti's style is too elaborate, obscure, and his ideas at times just short of the obscene.

ROUTH, JAMES. "Parallels in Coleridge, Keats, and Rossetti," *Modern Language Notes,* XXV (1910), 36. Denies any influence of Keats on Rossetti.

SHAIRP, PRINCIPAL. "Aesthetic Poetry: Dante Gabriel Rossetti," *Eclec-*

tic Magazine, XCIX (September 1882), 351. Finds fault in Rossetti's lack of nobler sentiment and manlier thought.

SHARP, WILLIAM. *Dante Gabriel Rossetti: A Record and a Study.* London: Macmillan and Company, 1882. Worthwhile examination of the poems, ballads, and sonnets.

SHINE, HILL. "The Influence of Keats on Rossetti," *Englishe Studien,* LXI (May 1927), 183–210. Sees a definite influence here in concept, style, and idea.

SPURGEON, CAROLINE F. E. *Mysticism in English Literature.* Cambridge: Cambridge University Press, 1922. Looks at Rossetti, along with Shelley, Keats, Browning, and Patmore in regard to the cult of Beauty.

SWINBURNE, ALGERNON. "Poetry of Dante Gabriel Rossetti," *Fortnightly Review,* XIII (May 1870), 551–79. Enthusiastic review of the Rossetti 1870 volume; profuse in statement, effusive in praise.

TISDEL, FREDERICK M. "Rossetti's *House of Life,*" *Modern Philology,* XV (September 1917), 257–76. Important study in the dating of Rossetti's *House* sonnets.

TROMBLY, ALBERT E. "Rossetti Studies: Craftsmanship," *South Atlantic Quarterly,* XVIII (July 1919), 211–21. Sees Rossetti as the greatest sonnet writer in English.

TURNER, ALBERT M. "Rossetti's Readings and His Critical Opinions," *Modern Language Association,* XII (1927), 465–91. Thorough study of Rossetti's readings.

WALLER, R. D. *The Rossetti Family: 1824–1854.* Manchester: Manchester University Press, 1932. Valuable study of the influences of Dante and Italian poets in Rossetti's early work.

WAUGH, EVELYN. *Rossetti, His Life and Works.* London: Duckworth, 1928. One of the first important studies to scrutinize the psychological aspects of Rossetti's life and works.

WINWAR, FRANCES. *Poor Splendid Wings: The Rossettis and Their Circle.* Boston: Little, Brown, and Company, 1933. Readable biography, but not one of the more reliable ones.

YEATS, W. B. *Essays and Introductions.* New York: Macmillan Company, 1961. An important collection of Yeats' essays (1896–1937) which sets forth his philosophy of poetry and drama. His "Art and Ideas" (1913) comments on Rossetti.

Index